Non-Profit Turnaround

How to Rescue a Failing Organization

Craig Copland

Published by:
Conservative Growth
1101 30th Street NW
Washington, DC 20007

Cover by Rita Toews

ISBN-13: 978-1481069434

ISBN-10: 1481069438

To friends and colleagues at Habitat for Humanity International with whom I have been honored to be associated for the past decade. Habitat for Humanity is an organization that does not need to be turned around. It is a wonderful example of how a non-profit organization should be run - with integrity and effectiveness.

A special dedication goes to the "three women with laptops and cell phones" who established Habitat throughout Europe and modeled how a small, capable, and determined group of individuals can bring passion and efficiency to a good cause.

Other books by Craig Copland:

2012 Conservative Election Handbook

Fundraising for Conservatives

The Myth of Wilderness Experience

CONTENTS

Acknowledgments

My basic understanding of the organizational management of non-profits came from my father, James. E. Copland. At the time of his retirement he was serving as the Vice-President Finance of Sears, when it was still the greatest mercantile organization in the world. His real passion, however, was for the numerous Christian organizations on whose boards he served as a volunteer. He expected all of them to be operated effectively and efficiently and never to lose sight of the children, families, and communities they were established to care for.

Over the past forty years I have been privileged to have been associated with many non-profit organizations. Some were models of excellence. Others were in trouble and needed help. All of them were led by people who sincerely wanted to help their fellow human being and make the world a better place. I have learned from all of those wonderful people, and I am humbly grateful for their contribution to my life.

Chapter One – Introduction

You are an employee or a board member of a non-profit organization.

Your organization does not exist to make money. It exists *to make a difference.*

You and the others you work with believe in your mission. You care about what you are doing. It's important, rewarding. It has meaning.

A few years ago your organization seemed to be healthy and growing. Your income was climbing. You were adding more staff. You were enthusiastically planning and launching more activities, events, and programs. You were causing changes in the lives of the people you served and the cause to which you are dedicated. It was all looking good.

Somehow, that changed.

First the rate of growth slowed down. Then for a few years you just held your own and stayed flat.

For the past several years your income has fallen. Important programs that you had planned, that were a part of your vision for the future, have either been postponed or cancelled. Hiring of new staff has been frozen. Staff who left recently have not been replaced and that's causing frustration within the remaining team members. Those positions were significant to your team and the organization.

Over the past two years there has been an operating deficit in your finances. Your reserves are being depleted. You may be into an overdraft with your bank. If you are the CEO or CFO then there are times in the middle of the night when you wake up and worry about how you are going to meet your payroll. Your suppliers used to get paid on thirty days. That became sixty days. Then ninety. Now they are calling and saying that they may not be able to do any more work until they get paid.

You are seriously considering having to cut your payroll and will likely not re-new some of the contracts that are about to expire, even though the work those people do is important, and they've been doing a good job.

Your board is aware of the situation and is very concerned but do not seem to know what to do.

You've talked to a few fundraising consultants but they all want a guaranteed per diem payment and you simply do not have to cash to afford that.

Okay. So you're in trouble. You're not the first and will not be the last. Charities, political organizations, service clubs, fraternal associations, amateur sports groups, and every other type of non-profit, large and small, all have ups and downs. Just like many businesses, some will go out of business. Others will turn around and prosper.

This book explains how to turn around a struggling or failing non-profit and make it successful and effective once again.

The steps it tells you to take are not easy, but they work. I've seen it happen.

I have been involved with non-profit organizations since I was a high school student (hmm…that would be, umm, more than forty years ago). I have been a volunteer, staff member, CEO, board member, and board chair in a total of over thirty organizations. Some were large with multi-million dollar budgets. Others were small and entirely run by volunteers. I am quite sure I have made every mistake there was to make along the way. All I can hope for is that I learned from them.

I have concluded that there is no cause or organization which cannot be salvaged and made to become effective, but I have also recognized that most organizations in trouble are the authors of their own ruin and that they need to change their attitudes and change their actions hard and fast if they want to be of continuing use to those they claim to serve.

Some readers will skim the instructions given below and accuse me of being inhuman (it's happened), or even unethical (that too) because I am advocating the use of the same very hard-nosed tactics used in the business world to rescue corporations and make them profitable. I can only reply that when an organization is within a year or less of having to close its doors and stop helping those people it was founded to be of service to, then the truly unethical course of action would be to just let that happen. Ethical behavior demands getting tough. Today. Later you can lighten up. But for now, it's time to make changes.

And that's what this book will explain how to do.

There are five steps in turning around a failing non-profit They are:

1. Change your thinking.
2. Figure out what went wrong.
3. Cut your costs.
4. Generate immediate cash.
5. Fix things and start growing again.

The structure of the book follows these five steps.

Chapters two through five address the first four steps.

The second part of the book, chapters six through twelve, are instructions concerning fundraising techniques that will bring in cash quickly and continue to do so until your organization is out of trouble.

I fully appreciate how important it is to those in leadership positions in the non-profit sector - and I am assuming that if you are reading these words that that's who you are - to do what is good and right and of benefit to others. Conversely, it is exceptionally difficult for them to act in ways that they know will bring pain to others. Sometimes, in order to keep an organization and its services from dying you have to act in ways that will be very hard. Sometimes you just have to do it.

Just do what the book tells you to and a year from now you can throw the book away. You will not need it anymore. Your organization will have recovered.

Chapter Two - Change Your Thinking

If you are a leader in a non-profit organization then there are likely four changes in the way you need to think:

1. Start to think like the private sector has to.
2. Face the facts and stop fudging the figures.
3. Cut the fat.
4. Think Cash Flow.

Is there a fundamental difference in the way that those in the for-profit and non-profit sectors think about what they do?

After four decades of having a foot in both camps I've concluded that, yes, there is.

The first insight came years ago when I met a friend for lunch at his corporate office. He was a senior executive at the local plant of Caterpillar Inc. As I waited for him in the building lobby I picked up and started browsing through a copy of Caterpillar's annual report. On the front page was their mission statement. It read:

"Our mission is to maximize the financial return to our shareholders."

Hmmm . . . couldn't be much clearer than that. The introductory comments went on to add some required words about quality and customers, but the message was unmistakable – shareholders come first.

Caterpillar is a massive multi-billion dollar company, one of the Dow, with a market cap in excess of $55 billion. They are brimming with corporate talent and marketing smarts. So could they not have come up with something a little more high-sounding?

No . . . but *why?*

Because their board and management knew that without shareholders there would be no international publically listed company. If they were to have several successive years of decline with continuing losses, no dividends, and plummeting share price, their shareholders would not sit idly by and let the company collapse. Instead they would replace the board members, and the board would fire the CEO, and the new CEO would turf out the executives and find better ones, and the new executives would get rid of non-performing staff, and on and on until they all got it right.

What if the *beneficiaries* of your organization were its *shareholders?*

What if they could vote and elect board members whose job was to maximize the returns to *them?* Here's what would happen: boards that had presided over declining organizations would be tossed out of office. CEO's and directors of development who had demonstrated their inability to reverse a decline and produce growing net returns would be fired. Program directors who could not manage projects on time and on budget would be replaced.

And rightly so!

Because corporations are ultimately accountable to their shareholders they constantly undergo creative destruction and corporate re-structuring. Poorly performing ones go out of business or are absorbed by stronger ones. When necessary, they merge. Wisely managed ones grow, re-structure, and grow some more. It's happening all over the corporate sectors of the developed world and it's all designed to maximize profits and return to investors.

But it's not happening in the charity and non-profit sectors.

Why not?

Because boards of non-profits and charities are functionally accountable to no-one.

What I have observed over and over again is that board members and executives in the non-profit sector like to think of themselves as accountable to so-called *stakeholders*. But for the most part the people to whom they functionally do account are their donors, members, and boards of directors, *not* the people whose needs they are supposed to be serving.

If they did, if they understood that their mandate was to maximize the returns to the beneficiaries without whose needs their organization would not exist, the likelihood of non-profits or charities getting into a financial crisis would be much less. Probably it would disappear.

The first step then in changing your thinking is:

Start to think of your beneficiaries - the people or cause you claim to be supporting - as if they were your <u>shareholders</u>.

The next change in your thinking revolves around being honest with yourself, your staff, and your board, facing the facts, and quit massaging the figures.

Publically traded businesses are required by law to be transparent and honest with their shareholders. If they are facing material risks to their profits, they have to disclose them. If they expect to miss their targets then they have to issue profit warnings. They cannot cook the books or they end up going to jail (read: Enron *et al*).

Unfortunately for the people that non-profits and charities exist to serve, there are no such comparable penalties imposed for fudging the figures.

Of course nobody commits outright fraud and issues financial statements that are knowingly false. But there are ways of massaging the numbers that non-profits can get away with but which carry with them the seeds of destruction.

For example: A number of years ago I sat on the board of a local church and helped draw up the budget for the coming year. I included in the budget a standard allowance for the depreciation of our assets. The building infrastructure, interior furnishings, office equipment, instructional facilities, and the like all decline in value and inevitably have to be replaced. Unexpected repairs have to be made. Unexpected changes in government regulations regarding property and buildings have to be complied with. So it was standard accounting and budgeting practice in the church and in any other non-profit I had been associated with to include depreciation allowances in the budget and to write down assets according to normal straight line formulae.

At the time, however, the church had recently expanded its facilities and was not exactly flush with cash. Any additional projects were on hold.

Our new minister, with his freshly minted seminary degree and little experience with things not theological, could see that the projected income would not permit him to include a couple of his pet initiatives and the salary of an additional staff member (to whom he had already promised a job). So he immediately demanded that the depreciation allowance be struck out of the budget. I pointed out this it was just standard budgeting practice to make such an allowance. To which he replied that I was using standards from the secular business world and that these had no place in the Lord's work. Business practices, it seems, are lumped in with blasphemers, idolaters and fornicators. I rather thought that it had a lot more to do with GAPP than God, but by that point he was on to quoting Bible verses and had made it clear that the Almighty was on his side (unbeknownst to Himself).

Now my father had warned me never to argue with a preacher. "Once logic fails them they go for their memory verses and you can't win." So I backed off and quit that board. The church, as expected, encountered unexpected costs for which it was not at all prepared and entered a decade of financial turmoil.

Another organization, a major international child care aid agency, decided to run a cross-county bicycle trek. Enthusiastic bicyclists would be recruited and they would raise pledges from their friends and family. Corporate sponsors would be sought to make donations in return for publicity and naming opportunities.

Similar events had been carried out by other non-profits with great success and had delivered hundreds of thousands of dollars in net income. The director of development and the executive director were sold and spent months enthusiastically planning the event. An event management firm that had operated similar events for other charities was contracted to run the operations with all due care for health and safety. The route was planned. The camping locations were all reserved. A major publicity campaign was contracted and launched. The board was all onside and the board chair had signed on as a rider, extracting pledges from other board members. The feelings were great and the expectations were euphoric.

Then some bad things started to happen. They honestly expected to have to limit participation to one hundred riders and turn away the rest. But the registrations did not come rushing in. A couple of months before the start date only thirty people had signed up. Several of them were struggling to meet the mandatory minimum sponsorship pledge level.

The major corporate sponsor altered its contribution agreement and instead of providing the entire amount in cash cut that figure in half and provided the rest as in-kind goods, much of which was of limited value to the participants or the charity.

A week before the start date there were only twenty riders who had met their pledge requirement. Hard-nosed common sense would have demanded that the event be cancelled so that losses could be cut. But by that point too many people had way too much of their souls, egos, and expectations invested. The event went ahead.

Those who had failed to meet their pledge target were told to come along anyway. A few staff members were given time off their jobs and joined the ride. The director of development's retired father was given some minor responsibilities and a bicycle and joined the gang.

For those who participated the event was a fantastic experience. After three weeks of bicycling through some stunningly beautiful parts of the continent they arrived at the finish line, greeted by friends, family, the entire staff of the head office, and one or two members of the media. Everybody congratulated each other on what had been a wonderful adventure and accomplishment.

Financially it was a disaster. In hard cash terms instead of netting the budgeted quarter of a million dollars it lost three hundred thousand.

But no one ever really knew.

Why? Because instead of showing all income and expense on the current accounts, the organization announced that this was the first of similar annual events. They would do it again next year and the year after. So they capitalized as many expenses as possible and moved them off the income statement and over to the balance sheet. If the consulting firm cost one hundred thousand dollars then all the materials they produced would be used again for the following three years and so the expense on the books was reduced to twenty-five thousand and an asset booked on the balance sheet of seventy-five thousand. All the publicity materials and campaigns were similarly capitalized – even the cost of the bicycles and helmets that were purchased for the staff.

As a result the amount on the financial records indicated a few dollars in net income and the balance sheet had nearly three hundred thousand dollars of dubious assets added. The auditors allowed it, having been assured that these assets were going to be used for the next three years.

The following year a very scaled-down ride was held again. After that the idea was scrapped and the assets written off.

The organization survived but several hundred thousand dollars that should have gone to children overseas never got sent.

Nobody likes being the bearer of bad news and it is human nature to try to sugar-coat a gloomy message. It happens all the time. In the private sector a corporation will always try to put a brave face on bad news, but ultimately they have to deliver the truth. Within non-profits a CEO has to be truthful in his or her reports to the board, but the board is under no compulsion to pass the message along. There are, by definition, no investors or shareholders in a non-profit who have to be truthfully informed. The bad news all too often never gets out of the boardroom.

Even more likely is the failure to face up not just to bad news but bad forecasts. Publically listed companies cannot legally give sales and profit forecasts to the public and their shareholders that are optimistic beyond the point of being truthful. If they know that they are going to miss their profit target they are required by law to disclose.

Again, no such discipline is applied to the non-profit sector. Budgets are routinely overly optimistic. If a VP of sales submitted a figure to a company budget that indicated a growth of twenty-five percent over the previous year and then failed to deliver on it, he or she would soon be looking for another job. But this type of pie-in-the-sky forecasting happens all the time in non-profits and people get away with it.

As a consultant I once sat in on a meeting in which the senior staff of the national office of a large and very respected international non-profit were presenting their budget and plan for the coming year to representatives of the international headquarters.

The presentation was very well-handled. Great visuals. Extensive documents. It looked as if a lot of homework and preparation had been done. There was one problem. When you added it all up, they were predicting that their top line income would double in one year. In a young and vigorous organization that's not impossible but it still seemed highly optimistic.

On the expense side of their budget they had shown a major increase in their payroll and planned to add several new staff positions. The increased costs were well within the amounts available according to their income budget.

I started asking questions.

For every line item showing the various streams of income they produced itemized work-up items with numbers attached. Every item seemed reasonable. The major corporations that were expected to donate all had an income figure attached. The various chapters of the organization were all showing levels of contributions that seemed achievable. The direct marketing lines seemed to be within the industry standard. So far so good.

Then I asked if I could see the previous year's comparable line item income report. That's when I realized that most of the income being shown was new income. The corporations and chapters that were listed had no history of having given in the past or if they had, never to the level that was being shown, reasonable though those new levels were.

When I challenged this way of constructing a budget I was informed that every one of these numbers was within reach and that collectively they could be achieved. Furthermore, they had prayed about these numbers and had a very strong conviction that they needed to exercise faith and leave some part of their results up to God for His intervention in response to their faith.

Hard to argue with that. My response was that allowing God to participate and deliver a twenty percent increase in overall income was more than enough faith and that a one hundred percent jump went beyond the bounds of faith and into fantasy. My theology was not appreciated.

In the end they achieved something closer to a very respectable fifteen percent growth. Fortunately they did not actually commit to the full list of new hires but they still faced a financial crunch later on the next year and had to get an unbudgeted subsidy from the international office in order to meet their program commitments.

None of the three examples I have given above – eliminating depreciation, moving items to the balance sheet, and faith-based budgeting – would survive in a publically listed corporation, yet they all happened in the non-profit sector.

They are all points along to way to financial ruin. If you are in a tight spot financially do not try to weasel out of it by sweeping your real expenses under the carpet. They will emerge to bite you. There are reasons for GAPP. Stick to the same type of financial rigour as would be required in the private sector. Fudging figures may not be illegal but ends up being a really expensive thing to do.

The second change in the way you think requires that you never fudge your figures.

The third way to start to change your thinking is to make a habit of looking for the fat, and cutting it.

During the past forty years I have been inside the offices of countless non-profit organizations. A while ago I was head-hunted for the position of CEO at a major Canadian aid agency dedicated to the needs of impoverished children in poor countries. I met in the organization's head office with the search committee of their board. The office was in a very upscale building in a very upscale part of town. It had abundant floor space and tasteful furnishings and, to my surprise, relatively few staff per square foot. Several staff who appeared to be twenty-somethings did not just have their own desk and cubicle, they had their own private offices.

During the interview most of the probing questions were some version or other of "How would you protect and enhance the experience of the volunteers of this organization?"

Huh?

The organization had established a network of self-appointing and perpetuating cells of volunteers across the country. Members of those cells ascended through the network and eventually became national board members. It was required of every board member that he or she had served at least two years as a volunteer cell member before they could be eligible to be a member of the board. Leaders of local cells and board members were involved in a constant schedule of consultations and meetings. They travelled not only all over the country but made numerous visits to the developing world so that they could have a first-hand look at the work that was being done by their field staff and indigenous partners.

What really bothered me about all this was not the level of poverty tourism or even the fact that this type of board recruitment was a sure way to keep highly qualified and effective potential members off the national board. It was that this organization's leaders clearly perceived that the people to whom they were responsible were their fellow volunteers, and not the children and families in Africa, Asia and Latin America that they were supposed to be serving.

Not surprisingly, the organization was in decline. They had way too much fat in their operations and most of it was self-indulgent towards the board members and other volunteers. I obviously did not answer their care-and-feeding-of-volunteers questions the right way and was not offered the job. Probably a good thing for all concerned.

What they really needed was to start seeing the fat for what it was and getting rid of it.

The most common source of fat in the non-profit sector is unnecessary employees, and it is always the most difficult to get non-profit leaders to accept. However, seeing this situation as *fat* is a necessary part of changing your thinking.

Several years ago I was asked to assist a major national health charity that was in dire straits. They were over a quarter of a million dollars in debt and continuing to lose money every quarter. The previous year they had cut their funding to medical research to almost zero. Their bank was watching their every move and starting to impose controls. Had they not been a respected national charity the bank would have closed their doors and pushed them into receivership.

After chatting with their staff for an afternoon it was immediately obvious to me that they had way too many people on payroll. They were all good people and were working hard, but some were working hard at finding things at which they could work hard.

So I immediately suggested to the executive director that he had to cut his payroll.

"No. We can't do that. Those are loyal employees that have worked here for a long time. I believe that as a charity dedicated to human welfare, we have to model inside our organization what we would like to see the world be like outside of our walls."

If I were in his position I would have felt the same way. There is nothing worse than having to terminate the employment of someone you have worked closely with for many years and come to know as a friend. When I have had to fire people it has been a devastating personal experience both for me and the one I had to terminate. It's no fun.

But . . . it had to be done. I sympathized with the executive director but those unnecessary personnel were costing the organization in excess of $200,000 a year. And that was money that should have been going to medical research. And if they didn't start to make tough cuts soon, nobody would have a job. They would be bust.

We toss epithets like *hatchet man* or *Chainsaw* at CEO's or board members who make significant cuts in staff, and we immortalize events as a *Saturday Night Massacre* when five or more staff are laid off at one time. To be "fixated on the bottom-line" is usually an insult term in the non-profit sector.

Most of us are drawn to the non-profit sector in part because we want to work in a milieu where people are treated with respect, not as expendable automatons. We expect people in *humanitarian* organizations to be *humane*. So it does not come easily to us to be tough minded, getting rid of those people who are not producing and putting pressure on those who are to do more.

Or worse, getting rid of good people who *are* producing but who we just can't afford to employ any longer.

More on cutting payroll in a later chapter. For now, it's enough to note that some things have to change. Or as the Italian novelist Giuseppi di Lampedusa wrote a few years back:

"If we want things to stay as they are, things will have to change."
Giuseppi di Lampedusa, in *The Leopard*

The third change in your thinking then is – see the fat and cut it.

And the final suggestion for ways to change your thinking:

Think Cash Flow

Annual income twenty pounds, annual expenditure nineteen, nineteen six, result happiness. Annual income twenty pounds, annual expenditure twenty pounds ought and six, result misery.

Mr. Micawber in *David Copperfield*

A few years ago I attended the International Fund Raising Conference in the Netherlands. A very highly respected fund-raising consultant and author offered a small group table seminar to discuss his particular approach to "relationship" fund raising. He opened his talk with the comment:

"If you think that fund raising is about money then you've got it all wrong."

Since I am occasionally tempted to be iconoclastic I just had to ask him:

"Have you ever been the CEO of a charity? Or the CFO? Have you ever been the individual responsible to employees and their families to meet a payroll, or to a board of directors to meet a budget?"

He acknowledged that he had not. Whereupon I proceeded to enlighten him as to the difference between being a director of development for an established multi-million dollar charity (his background) and the CEO of a start-up organization with no endowment, no reserve fund, no donor base, and no line of credit (my role at that time). In the former position you can afford to say that fund-raising is not about money. In the latter you do so at your peril.

When you're in trouble it's all about cash flow.

None of us enter a career in philanthropy expecting that we may at some point have to become obsessed with financial numbers. Too bad. Sometimes you have to be. The alternative is to cease to exist as a philanthropy for anybody.

The standard tool for watching your cash flow is a typical cash flow budget and report *that is updated daily – weekly at least.*

Most start-up non-profits close their doors for the same reason as most start-up small businesses do – because they run out of cash. They overestimated the amount of cash that would actually be available, they underestimated their costs, and when the cash did arrive it was always later than they had planned.

It is a truth universally acknowledged that fundraisers always expect more money to be received earlier than it ever does. That's okay. Fundraisers have to be optimistic positive people or they wouldn't last in that trade. But your CEO and your finance people cannot afford the luxury.

You or your accounting people need to lay out a fifty-two week spreadsheet and mark on it the dates and amounts when income is realistically expected to arrive and the dates and amount when expenses must be paid.

The best guide is your past experience. If an agency of government that provides you with grants has always taken three months to send the check in the past then there is no chance that it will send it within one month this year.

If your doubling date for your Christmas direct mail piece has always been three weeks after the mailing was dropped, then it will not suddenly get moved up to one week.

Non-profits that depend on grants from foundations and government programs are especially vulnerable to cash flow crises.

During the war in Bosnia the UK arm of the non-profit with which I was associated applied to the European Union for a large grant for their humanitarian relief program in the war zone and refugee camps. The application was approved and the organization launched its program. Time was of the essence since refugees were on the move and aid was needed immediately. But the money from the EU didn't arrive. Calls to Brussels received the same answer. "It's being processed." Meanwhile the organization had to meet the costs of payroll and field expenses, medical evacuation insurance, rental of lodging for their staff, fuel and transport of food, blankets, clothing, medicines, and other goods they were supplying. At one point they were just days away from running completely out of cash and having to shut down their program.

They avoided disaster by going to a bank that had dealt with other aid agencies in the past. They presented their documents confirming the approval of the grant. With the typical smug disdain that a Brit has for a Eurocrat the bank assured them that they had seen this situation many times before, that they were quite sure that the lazy French and Belgians would eventually send the funds, so of course they would advance them what was needed, with a stiff interest charge attached.

Risks to a non-profit's cash flow income from delayed grants and overly optimistic fundraising are all too common, but the most common expense peril is meeting payroll.

Payday is immutable. People who work for non-profits do not often have deep pockets. They simply cannot afford a delay in receiving their paychecks. They have to pay their rent, make their car payments, buy their family's food and so on. Even a delay from Friday to the following Monday creates a crisis for them.

Payment of some other expenses may be more flexible. Suppliers can be pushed out for another fifteen or thirty days. Even office rent can be paid a day or two or a week late. But the CEO and the head of finance simply must be on top of every date when salaries have to be paid. Doing so will allow you to project whether or not you are at risk of having your available cash fall below zero. If you can see that coming then you can take appropriate measures to avoid it. If you can't see it coming . . . you're in trouble.

.

Chapter Three - What Went Wrong?

Before you begin to implement fixes stop for a day or two and figure out what happened to get you into the mess in which you find yourself. Do not spend too long at this. In a financial crisis, time is of the essence. To over-simplify: there are two general types of financial crises - those that come as a shock and those that creep up.

The shockers:

A few years ago one of the largest and most vigorous Canadian foreign aid NGO's suddenly lapsed into receivership. We were told that it was the result of a perfect storm of really bad events.

They had grown quickly over the past decade. Their old location, which they owned, was now too small so they put it up for sale and prudently waited until it was sold before signing an offer to buy a new one. Almost all of their operating income came from grants from the Canadian government through CIDA (the Canadian equivalent of USAID). The grant agreements allowed them to allocate a portion of the income towards their administrative costs and they had budgeted according to the schedule of grants that had been approved.

But the sale of their old building fell through at the last minute and they were left with two properties, but only enough funds for one. At the same time the government announced a cutback on overseas aid money and CIDA moved quickly to implement those cuts. As a result the organization was notified that a couple of the grants they were approved to receive in the near future had been cancelled. A couple of the programs which were currently being funded had been extended from three years to five years with a corresponding stretching out of payments. Put together the events pushed them into a serious deficit. Their bank drew the line and stopped payment on their payroll checks. They went into receivership and into crisis mode.

In 20/20 hindsight maybe they should have had a much bigger reserve fund and certainly they shouldn't have had so many eggs in the government basket. But the convergence of events had been unpredictable. Bad things happen.

A few years before that time one of the largest and oldest child sponsorship agencies in the US had been harshly criticised in a couple of lines in a column in the *Washington Post*. Their director of development immediately sent out a defensive letter of explanation to their several hundred thousand child sponsors, ninety-nine point five percent of whom did not read the *Washington Post* and knew nothing of the criticism. In the heartland of America the old adage, "Where there's smoke there's fire" prevailed and twenty-five percent of the sponsors cancelled, forcing layoffs at the home office and a major retrenchment of projects around the developing world. In retrospect declaring your innocence to half a million people who don't know that you've been accused of anything was a really dumb move, but it happened. It was a shocker.

The creepers:

Situations where trouble creeps up slowly on an organization are much more common.

For example: I was once asked to meet with the board of a very fine community social service agency. For nearly twenty years they had received almost all of their funding from a government program and the directors had done a very responsible job as trustees of those funds, overseeing their expenditure in a prudent manner that would provide the best possible service to the community.

Then they were informed by the government agency that after a three year period their funding would be drastically cut and that they would have to develop their own sources of income from the community.

Sound familiar? All sorts of local community-based non-profits have had similar notices.

Acting responsibly the CEO and board worked on an RFP and sent it out to a number of charity consulting firms (time is passing). A few firms were selected. They prepared and made proposals to the board (more time) and one was selected. That group came back in a few weeks with a proposed plan (more time; money starts to be paid).

The plan was circulated to the board and approved. It was then put into action (seven months have passed). A case for support was written, reviewed, and revised (more time, more money). A marketing analysis was prepared and then an image design (more reviews, more revisions. 18 months has passed). Then research was undertaken to identify those corporations whose giving profiles best matched the profile of the client. A beautiful corporate social responsibility presentation package was designed, reviewed, revised, and produced (more money, more time). The firm proposed the development of a video and a CD but after much discussion these were turned down since program was already running over budget (one year left). The corporate campaign was launched and the packages were sent out to about one hundred major corporations that had demonstrated their support in the past by having made donations to similar agencies.

After three months two small donations had been received. Twenty letters praising the fine work of the charity but turning them down all the same had arrived. Another twenty or so had acknowledged receiving the package and given notice that it would be reviewed in due course. The consultants called these "warm responses". Another dozen or so had said that they were completely committed for this year but welcomed an application for the following year (more warm responses), and just under half of the targeted donors hadn't been heard from at all.

The consulting group proposed a Phase II noting that these campaigns were *long term investments*. This was not accepted. By then it was less than nine months to D-Day and over sixty thousand dollars had been spent with a return of less than ten thousand dollars in donations. Now they were facing a crisis. Everybody involved claimed to have acted responsibly but the crisis had crept up all the same. Some version of this story is getting repeated all over the country every day.

No doubt some of the responsibility for situations like this on can be blamed on bone-headed government bureaucrats and their political masters who like to think of themselves as humanitarian equivalents of angel investors that put up the start-up capital for a new venture and give organizations adequate time to become self-sufficient.

The problem with that approach, of course, is that community level non-profits do not locate themselves in and provide services to communities that will ever be capable of supporting those organizations. If those communities had that ability they would not need the help. These non-profits are based, by definition, in poor communities. Regardless of how much the members of those communities care about the organization and volunteer their time, they will never be able to raise enough money from the immediate community to cover the hard cash costs of the organization. Even if the lead time were five or ten years, the money just isn't there.

These things happen.

But you can't always blame the government. More disturbing are accounts of crises that have been festering for months if not years and have finally crossed the line.

A conservative religious educational institution in the Toronto area had been in operation for over a century. Almost every year for a decade they had had an operating deficit. All reserve funds had been used up. They were over a million dollars into a line of credit at their bank.

It was reported that at the board meeting immediately preceding their near death the directors spent most of their limited time debating about the person proposed as the upcoming commencement speaker. She was a highly respected religious leader but she was also an ordained minister. The conservative theological position of some board members did not go along with ordination of women and they claimed that having her as a commencement speaker would be giving tacit approval to that heresy. A brouhaha ensued and discussion of their financial crisis was squeezed to a few minutes at the end of the meeting. Within a few weeks the bank pulled the plug.

This is the *deer in the headlights* thing. Or call it *fiddling while Rome burns*, or the old *burying your head in the sand*. Choose your metaphor. It is the direct result of irresponsible oversight by management and board. It should never happen, but it does.

So go figure. If you're in a mess, take a hard look and ask how you got there. A shocker? Or a creeper? Wrought by circumstance beyond your reasonable control, or by just plain incompetence?

But figure it out fast, because time is marching on and with each passing minute you are sinking deeper. It's time to act.

Getting more specific:

We'll start with the **shockers**.

When a shocker hits an organization most often it is chalked up to bad luck or a series of unfortunate events. Actually, it is almost always the result of a failure to practice normal risk assessment and risk management.

Over the past couple of decades risk management has become a standard part of the planning and management of all types of operations and organizations. There now exist complicated mathematical models and an extended technical vocabulary as risk management is applied to massive engineering projects, international financial transactions, huge military projects, and so on. But there is also a level that comes down to common sense. That's the level that most non-profits need to adopt.

For beginners I recommend *The Complete Idiot's Guide to Risk Management,* (Annetta Cortez, Alpha Pub., 2010) – available from Amazon.com.

Doing basic risk assessment and management will help any organization avoid those events that blindside you and do very serious damage. If something really bad has happened to your non-profit, then take a day or two, look at what happened, and try to understand it from the perspective of risk.

When assessing risk you start by bringing your key people together and making a list of all the bad things that everyone can imagine could happen to you.

For each of those nasty events you assign two values, using any scale you want. One to ten works just fine. The first value given is the magnitude: i.e. just how devastating would it be if it actually happened. For example: a nasty letter about you in a local paper might be discouraging but not likely to have a serious impact on your operations. So maybe you could rate that as a One. However, a major accident involving a group of student volunteers serving on one of your overseas projects in which some were killed and others seriously injured would be very different. Accusations would made against you of negligence and lawsuits would be sure to follow that could put you out of business and mess up the lives of your senior staff for years to come. So that might rate a Ten.

Go through your whole list and assign a rating based on the relative impact.

The second value is the probability that the event might actually happen. A experienced group of your senior staff who have been around for a while can look at the list of possible bad events and come up with a rating of the likelihood of such an event occurring. For example: if there is someone in your local town who doesn't like your organization and likes to write letters to the local paper then the probability of such an event occurring in the near future is a sure thing. So give it a Ten. If you are constantly sending out teams of student volunteers to the Congo, or Afghanistan, or Cambodia then the chances of something bad happening are fairly high – maybe a Seven. But if you send out one team every two years and send them to Iceland then the probability becomes rather low – like, a Two.

Then you prioritize your risks. Those that are rated Ten-Ten – i.e. very likely to happen *and* have the potential to destroy your organization - go to the top of the list. Those that are One-One – i.e. very unlikely and even if they did happen there would be minimal consequences - go to the bottom of the priority list.

Risk management is the practice then of starting at the top of the list and putting in place whatever is needed to avoid the risk, to reduce the risk if it cannot be completely avoided, to share the risk by transferring it to another party through insurance, and to budget and prepare for those risks that are unavoidable and will have to be absorbed.

If a shocker has hurt your organization take a look at what happened and try to understand it in the context of risk assessment and management.

How probable was it that something like what did happen could have happened?

In retrospect, what might you have done to avoid the risk, or at least to have reduced its potential for harm?

Was there some sort of insurance that you could have purchased that would have shared the risk with an underwriter?

Should you have known that something like what happened was bound to happen someday, and could not be predicted or avoided? So should you have set aside reserve funds in order to absorb the impact?

Obviously, doing risk assessment after the fact is like closing the barn door after the horses have gone. But walking through the process will help your organization to understand what did happen to you, and to make sure that it never happens again.

A sobering story: An international Christian student organization had planned a retreat for some university students. Transportation had been arranged through a local bus company. At the last minute several more students wanted to come but the bus was full and the bus company would not take any more than the legally permitted limit. One of the staff, not wanting to turn the students away, contacted a friend who owned an extended mini-van and asked if it could be borrowed. Agreed. The staff member would drive.

The van was in a serious accident. One student was killed and two were badly injured, requiring extended hospital care, therapy, and the expectation of a lifetime of some type of physical discomfort and handicap. The families requested appropriate insurance compensation. The insurance company of the van owner refused. There was nothing in the owner's policy that remotely covered loaning it to a corporation for use in transporting students and using another driver.

So the lawsuit then came to the non-profit organization that was in charge of the event since they had authorized the borrowing and the driver. The organization's own insurance company also refused to pay, noting that while the event itself was covered nothing in the organization's policy covered transport using borrowed private vehicles driven by someone with only a standard driver's licence. So the organization was on the hook. They ended up paying out over half a million dollars, which was the negotiated amount that they agreed to in order to avoid a ruinously costly court battle.

Looking back, the organization should have had policies in place governing how it transported students and specifically prohibiting the type of last minute arrangement that took place. They also should have had far more extensive insurance policies that covered all possible disasters that could happen when holding student retreats.

Bad things happen. When they do, learn from them, and understand what happened and why. And then don't let them happen again.

Enough about trying to understand what happened when a shocker hit you.

Let's move on to the **creepers.**

How is it that some non-profits just bury their heads in the sand while disaster creeps up on them, then hit the tipping point, and find themselves in crisis?

From my experience, it is again the result of the failure of those non-profits to identify risks. Publically listed corporations are required by law to issue quarterly financial statements. As part of the MD&A component of those statements they are obligated to inform investors and potential investors of risks that could have an impact on the operations and profitability of the corporation.

Non-profits are under no such binding obligation and routinely fail to think about let alone speak about risk. They need to change.

The most common **creepers** are:

Aging of the donor base:

A few years back I met with a wonderful Christian organization that has been placing Bibles in hotel rooms for over a century. I observed that they depended almost entirely on direct mail for their income and concluded that the average age of their donors was now over fifty-five and likely closer to sixty. They acknowledged that the average donor was in fact seventy years of age and that hundreds of them were now dying every year and not being replenished by younger donors. Their donations were declining. You cannot stop demographics.

Note: this creeper is present in every non-profit that is overly dependent on direct mail.

Aging of the cause:

Donations to AIDS related organizations appear to have peaked in the late 1990's. Since that time the widespread availability of anti-retroviral drugs, the decline in infection rates, and the announcing of high levels of government funding have combined to bring about a continuing decline in donations from the public. The need is still staggering, especially in parts of the world like sub-Saharan African and the Caribbean, but in Europe and North America, where HIV-AIDS is no longer a death sentence, the aging of the cause has crept up on many organizations.

Payroll creep:

Fifteen years ago the European office of a highly respected international charity supervised the work of the organization in over a dozen countries across Europe and central Asia. The office was run by four staff. They lived out of suitcases, on and off airplanes, and in economy grade hotels - and the work somehow all got done. Today that same office has a staff of forty people. The territory has expanded by a couple more countries and the work has become much more sophisticated. And yet not all that many more families are being helped.

Studies of management and administration have noted that if left unchecked a bureaucracy tends to grow, like a virus, at a universal rate of about seven percent a year regardless of the size of the work load and regardless of the type of organization. This can be deadly.

Too much dependency on government grants:

Many non-profits chase government grants and are successful in securing large amounts of money to fund their very worthy projects. Government priorities change however. What the government wanted to fund one year may change the next and the non-profit may find itself no longer on the recipient list. If all that a non-profit did was to add contract staff as required for each government funded program and let them go when the program finished, this would not be a problem.

But that's not what they do. They add full-time employees not just for the program but as support and administrative staff necessary for the effective management and reporting on the project. They expand their office floor space, software, and equipment. They upgrade their communications systems and so on. Then they are stuck with these additional costs when a project is not renewed.

A few years back I met in Belfast, Northern Ireland, with an agency that had developed an exceptional program aimed at reconciliation between the Catholic and Protestant communities. It was generously funded by the UK government and they were being pressed to do even more of their good work. I complimented them on their success and excellent programs but cautioned them that the single most fickle source of funds for non-profits was politically motivated government grants. They had not built a donor base of individuals, corporations, or foundations outside of the government but they fully expected that the funds would continue to be provided for years to come. After all, the *Troubles* had been going on for over thirty years, and they weren't about to end anytime soon.

Then the unexpected happened. The Catholics and the Protestants reconciled. They stopped killing each other. They more or less agreed to get along. So the government funds for reconciliation projects wound down quickly. The organization closed its doors.

Continuing operating loss:

If with each passing year the income/expense statements show an operating loss, that money has to come from somewhere. First the working capital is depleted. Then the reserve funds start to diminish. Funds that were invested in longer-term deposits get cashed in and moved over into current accounts. The situation is called "temporary," a result of a disappointing response to a recent appeal letter. But that response was analysed and the next appeal is sure to be much better. The programs are going well and no one in the office or on the board can imagine stopping any one of them just to save money. The staff are an exceptionally enthusiastic and dedicated team that obviously care about each other and love working together for their cause. Letting any one of them go would be devastating. So nothing happens. The organization slowly but steadily drifts towards the waterfall. And then one day the bank refuses to honor the payroll checks.

Exciting events become a bore:

Some of you are old enough to remember the *Miles for Millions* marches that were held in many cities during the late 1960's and 1970's. Hundreds of thousands of teenagers walked for thirty-five miles in a single day and raised millions of dollars for charities helping children in Africa. For students it was the event of the year. You just had to be part of it. A few years later the number of participants had dwindled to a few thousand – a ninety percent drop from the peak. It was costing the organizers more than they were getting in donations. The walk ended.

Most events have a cycle. They grow. They peak. They decline. Hanging on too long and depending on them for essential net income is always dangerous.

Timing can kill you:

If you have committed to starting a program or project in June, fully expecting that the funds will be in place, and then the grant, or event, or estate gift on which you depended for funding is postponed until October, you could be in trouble. By the end of the year the money you need will be there but when you need it, it's not. So what do you do? If you have sufficient working capital you're okay. If you have reserve funds into which you can dip and later replenish, then you will get through. But if you are a relatively young agency and have neither working capital nor reserves, you're in a fix. If at all possible, the project will have to be postponed, often with seriously negative results. If it cannot be postponed then it will have to be cancelled, usually with even worse results.

Ruinous liability of matching grants:

If you received a $600,000 grant from a government agency or a foundation you would normally be thrilled. But if it stipulated a 3:1 matching formula then you just incurred a cash liability of $200,000.

Worse yet if it was 2:1 or even 1:1. If you don't have the cash available when you need it, you have a problem. Again you will have to use your reserve funds, and if you do that too often they eventually run out. Very few non-profits have the common sense to refuse a large grant because of the match requirements, especially if a dedicated staff team have spent months developing the successful application.

Gifts-in-kind liabilities:

The same problem applies to gifts-in-kind. A group of hospitals may donate several million dollars' worth of medicines and medical equipment that you know would be a godsend to your overseas partners. However, such valuable goods will have to be stored until you are ready to send them. That costs. The storage facility will have to be secured not only from smash and grab thieves, but from staff, contractors, and delivery people who might want to help themselves. If your beneficiary partners overseas cannot manage the whole shipment all at once, then you will have to continue to store the goods. More costs. If the goods have to be sorted and divided up and sent out in different shipments over a period of several months then you have to pay for continuing secure storage. Eventually you will have to pack the shipments and send them. If there are medicines that have expiry dates on them then you might end up with pharmaceuticals that can no longer be shipped anywhere but have to undergo safe medical disposal. More costs. Staff time has to be allocated to all of the above activities. You can have a serious hit on your cash just looking after and shipping all your wonderful gift-in kind. It can hurt.

Poisonous personnel:

Non-profit organizations, be they related to churches and religious causes, the environment, poverty reduction, children in need, wild animals or pets, health, the arts . . . whatever, seem to be a magnet for employees and volunteers who are impossible to work with. You know the type. He or she is passionately committed to the cause, comes in early and leaves late, always ready to work overtime or on weekends, and always speaking on behalf of the beneficiaries or defending the interests of the cause. Yet they have serious personality issues that make them extremely difficult to get along with.

They can be arrogant and prone to making demeaning insults. They will twist and misrepresent what others have said or written. They will say one thing to your face and another behind your back. But they may be politically cunning and ingratiate themselves to board members, or executive staff, or major donors. You cannot fault the quality of their work. It is always done well and on time. It is virtually impossible to get rid of them.

Over time, however, those who have to work alongside them begin to hate coming to work. Eventually they quit and find another worthy cause to support where people have a good time together. Over time, there is a constant turnover of excellent employees and key positions are always having to be advertised and filled. A stable, committed, and competent staff are critical to the growth of any organization and progress is limited if you are constantly churning through good people. This situation is often accompanied by gradual decline in the organization and it is a very tough one to fix. Good luck.

Good old fashioned incompetence at the top:

Way back in 1969 Lawrence Peter articulated what he called *The Peter Principle*. It stated that "employees tend to rise to the level of their incompetence." Much has been written about the effective use of employees since that time but I have yet to see anyone refute this maxim. Within non-profits it is often directly connected to the founder (almost always a male, sometimes along with his wife). A visionary, passionately committed, charismatic individual starts a non-profit and by sheer force of personality and hard work builds a organization that ends up with a budget of millions of dollars and a large staff of employees. The founder is universally respected by the public. His personal life is exemplary. His closeness to the mission of the organization is unmatched.

But . . . he is just not a capable manager of a multi-million dollar business. He is totally unskilled in professional management of human resources and continues to hire and promote friends and family. He has established principles and practices that may have been useful in helping the organization grow but now are no longer appropriate yet he won't hear of changing them. He authorizes major expenditures and program initiatives without any standard budgeting and planning. The board members are his close personal friends who are dedicated to supporting him but are small business people or local professionals with no experience at all governing a large corporation. Eventually and inevitably the organization gets into trouble.

These are just the creeper situations that I have seen over the years as I have watched once thriving organizations slowly decline, or I have learned about when called into to help a group that is now in trouble. You may have seen other situations that I haven't. Regardless of whatever the creeping situation, you need to first understand it, and then fix it.

What you cannot do is just ignore a creeper until it becomes a disaster. Somebody has to speak up and say "Whoa. We have a problem here."

Chapter Four - Cut the Fat

To turn around cash flow you do two things: decrease costs and increase net income.

Cutting costs comes first:

Why? Do the math. In the non-profit business it is very difficult to implement any new fund-raising program which will generate a lot of additional new net income in less than three months. Most programs require a front-end investment, and almost any new activity that will produce gross income will only net out ten to fifty percent in the first year, at best. Options for rapid growth of net income are limited (see below for those things you *can* do). But cutting costs will produce an increase in cash flow overnight. So, where do you start cutting?

Payroll:

For nearly twenty years I was in positions where I experienced the joy of hiring people and the agony of firing those which didn't work out. Of all the things I did over those years, firing somebody was the absolute worst. Call it what you want - "layoff due to economic conditions", "termination due to re-structuring" - it doesn't matter much. I still had to meet with someone and tell him or her that the job was ending. I *hated* doing it. So I procrastinated. I set deadlines for improvement in achievement which I subsequently extended. I paced the office and warehouse floor long after all the employees had gone home trying to think up ways I could *save* a position, or re-assign someone to a role where they might do better. I felt enormous guilt knowing that most of the terminations I had to do were my own fault for not doing a thorough job recruiting, screening, and checking references before hiring. Then I would give severance packages way above the industry standard so I'd feel less guilty.

The day a man started to cry in front of me when I told him that he could not come back in on Monday morning was the day I just about packed it in myself and quit. Most of you reading this have gone through similar traumatic experiences, right? Working together for a good cause is supposed to be positive, empowering, liberating, fun. So having to terminate people is the last thing you ever want to do. Well, guess what? When you're in trouble it is likely the first thing you have to do. So suck it up and do it.

You have to ask yourself, "Could this non-profit be run with fewer employees?" The answer is almost always a resounding "Yes." Could it be run if salaries were cut by ten or fifteen percent? Most likely, yes. Could it be run if the benefits, the pension contributions, or the vacations were cut way back? Almost always, yes. Could it be run by the most productive half to two thirds of the current staff working from eight in the morning to six at night? Probably yes, at least for six months. Could you invoke a temporary layoff of some staff for up to thirteen weeks? Sure. Is any executive *still* using a secretary to transcribe hand-written letters and reports, take dictation, book appointments, or answer phone calls? Then spend a few dollars and get that executive a teach-yourself-to-type book and some contact management software, and give him (it's almost always a male) five minutes instruction on how to use voice mail. And then cut out the clerical position.

It is very likely that if you are struggling financially then your payroll has almost certainly crept upwards. It is also almost certain that you could operate your organization with twenty-five percent fewer people and still do quite well.

Payroll costs within charitable organizations steal up over time at a rate faster than increased net income. Start cutting some today. It beats having to cut a lot more tomorrow. Do it.

Professional fees:

Lawyers. Accountants. Consultants. Terminate any agreement which has somebody getting paid on a retainer even when they're not doing anything. They, or somebody else, can always be contracted again later. Bring accounting services in-house as much as possible.

One board I know of decided that they were going to exercise exceptional due diligence and required that the charity's statements be drafted in-house and then sent out to a big five accounting firm for review, *every month*. The fee was over six thousand dollars a month. A kid fresh out of book-keeping school armed with *Simply Accounting* or *Quick Books* could have generated a perfectly acceptable set of monthly statements. Integrity and accuracy in accounting are important, but that was overkill.

Similarly, when I started up an international relief charity I took our audit to one of those firms with a double name (now triple) so we could have the legitimacy their name would provide to our donors. Guess what? Ninety-nine percent of the donors could not have cared less. And guess what again? They wanted three times more than the local independent firm we eventually went to.

Do you have consultants helping your Board to "define your mission" or "think strategically" or "articulate policy development procedures" or whatever? Get rid of them. Get rid of any consultant to whom you cannot ascribe direct and continuing credit for improving your cash flow several times in excess of their fees. When you're flush with cash hire them back if you are still convinced that you really need them.

Facilities:

Do you own your office facility outright? If so, why? For a decade real estate in both the US and Canada has been a lousy investment. Better to sell the facility, lease it back and invest the difference in low risk securities. Even if you only have partial equity in a property this may make sense. Could you cram your staff into a third or a half of the space you are currently using and rent out the rest? Not for ever, but for now. Are you renting expensive downtown space when even stockbrokers are re-locating to the burbs?

Are you prepared to play hardball with your landlord? Have you tried going to him or her and saying, "Our non-profit organization is in a difficult financial position, so we are not going to be able to pay our full rent this month, so could you please donate the balance and we will provide appropriate documentation so that you can claim it for tax purposes?" Or, if you are already behind on your rent then go and with a straight face ask the landlord to forgive the back rent as a donation. Most landlords really do not want to throw charities out on the street and they would rather have the space occupied and paying at least something rather than sitting empty. Try it. The worst that can happen is that they say no.

Travel, conferences, and professional associations:

Have you bought a plane ticket lately for a trip within North America? Or stayed at a downtown hotel in a major city? Prices are way up. And all costs have to be paid in cash at the time they are incurred. If you're short of cash *stop travelling*. Communicate by e-mail or phone. Entire board meetings and board committee meetings can and should be held on conference call. Cancel all convention attendance even if it means losing your deposit. For the next six months one hundred percent of everybody's time is needed to turn your organization around.

How much time are staff members putting into professional associations or interest groups? The entire staff of one anti-poverty group I met with was spending a whole day every week meeting with similar activist groups in the city and surrounding area. They claimed it was very important to them to "make common cause," and "develop a coherent collective regional strategy and policies." I saw it as socializing and getting paid for it. Honestly, can you imagine all the marketing staff at Walmart getting together for a full day every week with their counterparts at Sears, Costco, and Home Depot to discuss issues common to major retailers? D'uuh? Let somebody else carry the torch for the shared cause for a while. Today *you* can't afford to. Tomorrow maybe.

Communications:

Internal and external newsletters, annual reports, brochures, reports, proceedings of conferences, videos, CDs and web sites - all these things are *costs*. They do not on their own generate net income. At best they may marginally support fundraising at a ratio of ninety-five cents on the dollar. (i.e. for every dollar spent on communications you would be very lucky to be able to point to even another five cents received in donations). When I started working with one client they were in the middle of producing their corporate CD. Several key staff had spent most of their time over the past three months on it. Somebody had convinced them that potential corporate donors would be so impressed by their coming to a presentation and plugging in their CD that all sorts of new donations would start flowing. Is there no end to naiveté? Their final product came out three months late and was obsolete within six.

Everybody wants a web site. Thousands of dollars are being spent on them. Some are actually beautiful to look at and a sheer delight to visit and navigate through. But how much additional income is any charity now collecting from its donors because they have spent a fortune on a web site? In the not too distant future the Internet will probably be a significant channel for acquiring net income for non-profits and we will all need sophisticated websites. Today, it's an unaffordable expense for anybody in trouble. Stick with basic.

Advice? If things are really tight put your entire communications staff on thirteen week temporary layoff. Have anybody on staff who can write a sentence and put it into a coherent paragraph write up a one page news brief every couple of months and stuff it into your donor receipts. Keep alive only those communications functions which can demonstrate an immediate enhancement to your net fundraising income. And please, interpret anything you hear which sounds like "Our purpose wasn't really to make money but to build awareness" as meaning "We failed to make any money."

Planned giving:

Do the math. An ideal prospect meeting is held with a couple who are both seventy years old and who have been volunteers with your charity for over thirty years. Their children are grown up. They want to remember you in their will and they indicate that they wish to designate a sum of $500,000 as a bequest. Like, how good does it get?

Here's the problem - according to standard actuarial tables for Americans and Canadians, at what age, on average, will the surviving spouse of a 70 year old couple who are healthy in 2013, die? Answer: age 94. So in the year 2037 your organization will get $500,000. Not much good if you are going to be out of business before the end of 2014. Planned giving programs are highly necessary for the long term health of those organizations that can afford to carry the investment until the program starts to make net income. If you are not in a position to make long term investments, don't bother. Either terminate the planned giving program completely and start it up again in a year or two (Mr.. and Mrs. Seventy-Year-Old will still be around); or transfer the staff to the securing of major personal gifts from individuals *today*.

Sorry. No offense to the planned giving professionals. But the average planned giving program takes about ten years to deliver more income than it costs. So today they're a cost and can be cut today. In the future your cash flow will be better. It's only a short term gain, you say? You're right. That's *exactly* what it is.

Any other costs:

What about phone, fax, postage, courier? Can they be replaced by email? Can you defer a capital expenditure even for three months? Can you renegotiate your rates with various suppliers? Have you ever tried?

One colleague of mine made a fortune for himself and his clients by going around to their suppliers and landlords and negotiating lower rates. He was a very good hard-nosed negotiator, but invariably he walked into situations where nobody before him had *ever even asked*.

Does anybody have a company car? Why? Are you paying for advertising which cannot be shown to be contributing directly to net income? Are you subsidizing staff lunches with an employee cafeteria or free employee parking? Whatever. If it can't be justified then out it goes.

Do it now. Do not initiate a broad-based consultation with every stake-holder. Do not hire a consultant. Do not wait. Make a list today of all possible cuts available and start slashing. If you succeed in your turnaround then some of the most painful cuts can possibly be restored. If you cease to exist then it's all over anyway.

Craig Copland

Chapter Five - Find Cash, Fast

Replace non-performers with those who produce.

The past few years have been very hard on all types of businesses. Tens of thousands of businesses, large and small, non-profit and for-profit, in all corners of the continent have gone under. So there is no shame in knowing that your non-profit organization has seen its income decline. The questions you have to ask and get answers for are "How much trouble are we really in compared to everybody else? How are we doing compared to our peers?" If your recent results are the same or better, then relax and recover along with the economy.

But what if your results have been significantly worse than other organizations like yours? What if your overall decline in income was over thirty percent but the average for your sector was only fifteen percent? What if you are continuing to decline while your peers have levelled off and have started to recover?

If you are in a serious crunch *and* your performance is substantially behind your peer group then it is quite obvious what is wrong.

You have a non-performing organization. Somewhere in your structure there are people who are just not up to snuff. You're carrying some non-performers somewhere.

If you are the board of directors:

If you are a member of the board then the first place to look is at your CEO.

Is it time to find a new one? Do you need to find someone who knows how to bring in the bucks?

Replacing a CEO is a very serious step for a non-profit. Often the incumbent has become the public face of the organization. He or she may have developed strong personal friendships with some of the board members. The employees will likely look up to him or her and cannot imagine working in the organization with any other person at the helm. The CEO may be a person of the highest integrity and passionately committed to the cause of the organization. The only problem is that he or she is just not sufficiently capable to keep to organization out of continuing financial decline.

So what do you do?

First, understand and accept that as directors of a corporation, or as trustees of a non-profit organization, you have a fiduciary duty to the organization that must take precedence over your personal friendship, loyalty, and respect for the CEO. This is not an easy thing to do. But if the alternative is to see the organization continue to slide towards bankruptcy then you have no choice but to act. You cannot sit idly by and let the organization fail.

However, the second question you have to ask is "Would replacing the CEO do more harm than good? Do we have someone else who can take charge and do a better job?" If you are not ready to replace a CEO then don't. Find some sort of alternative. Perhaps insist that a COO be recruited and installed who can do a better job of financial management and business administration. Or shift your CEO to a role more like Honorary President, or Global Ambassador, or something like that where he or she is still involved and communicating the cause of the organization to the public, but removed from day-to-day management.

Caution: I have seen three boards that replaced CEO's who were, in fact, doing quite a good job of managing their organizations and who were not in serious financial difficulty, but who were replaced under the guise of finance when the real reason was politics. In two cases there were executive members of the board who although not lacking personal net worth were unemployed at the time and longed for the CEO position. They engineered the dismissal of the CEO so that they could take the job. One was in turn removed from the CEO job three months later after the entire staff complained about her abusive personality, and the second immediately hired his very weird unemployable son and had his wife replace him on the board.

The third situation happened with a board that was made up both of highly qualified independent corporate types and representatives of the organization's chapters. At one board meeting where barely enough members showed up to make a quorum, the chapter representatives for once outnumbered the independent directors and voted to oust the CEO for reasons that were entirely political, in the sole interest of increasing the power of the chapters, and had nothing to do with the performance of the organization.

Conclusion? Be prepared to replace a CEO who cannot lead an organization out of financial decline, but proceed with caution.

If you are the CEO:

If you are the CEO and your net fundraising income has declined at a rate much below the industry average for the past two or three years then fire your director of development and replace him or her with someone who is better at running a set of fundraising programs.

Obviously no responsible leader of an organization can do a Donald Trump "You're fired!" stunt. But you most certainly can set reasonable targets for your leading development executive, do regular performance reviews, and provide whatever support and assistance appropriate in your role as CEO. But if the person you have leading your fundraising programs consistently fails to meet reasonable targets and cannot deliver agreed upon results, you need to look into the possibility of replacing him or her.

There is a reason that there is a constant churn of directors of development in the non-profit sector. In many ways it's like being a baseball manager. There are a large number of people working in the field but very few real stars. Take a look at the job postings in the *Chronicle of Philanthropy* or *Non-Profit Times* (or on *Charity Village* if you're in Canada) and you will see that every day there are hundreds of agencies looking for good fundraisers. If you have reached the inescapable conclusion that your organization will never get out of the hole with your current development person, the start looking for somebody who will make the difference you need.

If you are the Director of Development:

Except for very small organizations, most non-profits today will have several fundraising staff. Typically there will be one responsible for direct marketing, one for special events, one for corporations, one for major gifts, one for planned gifts, and so on. If any of your staff have been in place for two years or longer without being able to meet reasonable goals in net income then you need to terminate and replace them. If their sector of responsibility has actually declined at a rate much worse than the industry average for two years running, then fire them quickly and get somebody in place who knows how to make money.

Unfortunately nobody can fire an incompetent charity board of directors. Too bad. And things usually have to be really drastic for a board to vote to remove a sitting member. But if you are facing a financial crisis you could select those directors whom you know to be the most competent, *whom you would vote to be your representatives on the board if you were a beneficiary of the charity,* and place them on the Turnaround Team (see below) and give them special powers to act until the turnaround is successfully underway.

Start asking for money and start *with the board:*

In his classic book, Dale Carnegie relates the story of the mother who paid a visit to the renowned child psychologist and asked him, "Please tell me, doctor, how can I teach my children to have good manners?" The good doctor replied, "Why, don't you know, madam, there are three simple rules which, if followed, absolutely guarantee that your children will have excellent manners." "Oh, please tell them to me right away!" "Well the first one is 'By example', and the second one is 'By example', and the third one is 'By example'."

If your board expects the public to give to the cause for which it is responsible then they lead **by example.** *Every* board member should give donations appropriate to his or her income level and situation. Ideally they should be major donors or sustaining monthly donors.

The next thing every board member should do is take responsibility for arranging meetings with prospective donors with whom they are in personal contact. This should be happening all the time anyway even in a financially healthy charity. Rule of thumb - five meetings a year per board member. That works out to one every two months with the summer off. If you are in a crisis, or even just in a start-up situation, the quota goes up to one or more every month. The board member sets up the meeting either with an individual or with a corporation with whom he or she has some direct personal contact. They accompany the staff member (CEO, director of development, or corporate gifts officer, depending on the potential of the gift) and they say, "I am personally supporting this wonderful cause and I would like you to join with me in doing so. Our CEO here is going to tell you all about what the charity is doing and how you can help."

That's all you need to do. Just start doing it.

When an organization is facing a financial crisis every board member follows the same orders – *you give, you get, or you get lost*. Actually that rule should apply to every board member all of the time, rain or shine. If you had applied it in the past you would not be in a financial crunch now.

Millard Fuller, the founder of Habitat for Humanity, told a Habitat gathering a while back (try to hear this in a deep Georgia drawl), "Y'all know something . . . There's just two types of people out there in Amurrrica. There's folks we tell about Habitat and ask them to help us, and there's folks we don't. An' you know somethin'? Why we get a whole lot more help from the first group than the second."

Back to the community agency I referred to above who had spent a lot of money and wasted a lot of time trying to put a fundraising program in place. In fifteen minutes of *pro bono* time I told them all they needed to know. Simply put it was, "Take whatever you've got now, get off your backsides (okay, so I didn't say "backsides") and get out there and start asking for money. And if you want to be any good at it then you better lead by example." That particular group warmly thanked me for my time, assured me that they would do just that and to the best of my knowledge they went and did it.

However, in two other situations I said the same thing. Most of the heads around the table nodded in agreement. But there was at least one individual in each group who responded to my comments as if I had told them to commit some sort of humiliating felony. "The reason I joined this organization," said one, "is because nobody ever tries to get other people to give money. I hate it when I'm asked for money. It makes everybody feel uncomfortable. We should never have to do that!" And he was *really* serious. In the other group the president of the board, a teacher with independent income on top of her salary, replied, "I'm sorry, but *time is money* and I give my time, so I don't feel like I should have to give my money too." I asked her whether she could use her *time* to pay the office rent, or the salary of the staff. To no avail, she just repeated "Time is money."

Well, dear board members, if you're expected to set up an meeting with one of your contacts this month and you put it off to next month, then time *is* money. But otherwise, especially if your non-profit is financially strapped, *cash* is money and that's all there is to it. So cough up according to the limit of your means and keep coughing up and keep asking others to do so to.

Then get the staff moving:

The same rule applies here. *Those who don't ask, don't get.*

A few years ago I made a huge mistake when I offered the job of corporate gifts officer to an incredibly fine man who was a good friend to a number of my staff. He had recently become unemployed as a result of a company merger. For two years he sat in his office and came up with every excuse in the book as to why he was not making cold calls, not getting out to do asks, and not hitting the budget targets. He was just a great guy in the wrong job.

Eventually I let him go and hired a young woman who had just come from working for five years in straight commission sales. She wanted to do something to help children in need. Before starting the job she read up on what we did. Her first morning she opened a bunch of donor files. That afternoon she started making phone calls. By the end of the week she was going to her first meetings. The results were stunning. We went from way behind budget to way over in a few months. In two years she alone had made a difference of over $15 million dollars.

She had never heard of a CFRE designation. She had never attended a single seminar on trends in corporate giving or the ethics of philanthropy. She taught me that getting in major gifts was much more a result of selecting leads, making phone calls, setting appointments, making presentations, closing sales, hitting quotas and growing accounts than about all the fundraising theories I had ever read. Perhaps when you are well-established, major individual and corporate gifts can be about *relationships* and *friend raising*. When you're starting up or when you're facing a cash crisis getting gifts in the door is about sales. Pure and simple. The "ABC's of sales" - *Always Be Closing*.

In tough times, set quotas. A CEO should be attending at least one or two meetings a week making asks; a director of development two to three meetings; and a major or corporate gifts officer at least four. Support staff can assist in making appointments, doing some basic background checks, and putting a simple package together for taking to the meeting. Your research does not have to be worthy of being published in *Lancet*. Your printed materials or PowerPoint do not need to be eligible for industry awards. There may well be some self-appointed experts in the philanthropy sector who will look down their noses at your less than perfect ways of going about things. Well, so what?

I'm reminded of the story of Dwight L. Moody, the 19th century American evangelist, who was heading off to England for a revival campaign. He was informed that some of the English clergy were critical of his activities and thought them to be rather crude and unsophisticated methods of evangelism. To which he replied, "I guess I'm happier about the evangelism I'm doing than the evangelism they're *not* doing."

The same thing applies to fundraising. It's about shoe leather. It's about elbow grease. It's about sales. It's about getting out and doing it every day. A simple, unpolished campaign with a modicum of research and modest materials which *is* happening every day, is always better by far than a thoroughly planned one with dazzling materials which *isn't* happening.

I am constantly amazed when talking with non-profit clients at the number who haven't made a new ask in the past week or even in the past month. Like, do they think money is going to fall out of the sky? When in trouble, set quotas for appointments for everybody, lead by example. Get out and ask. Not having done so in the past likely accounts for much of why you're in a financial crisis today. If between your board members and staff you could go and ask thirty or more people or corporations *every month* for money, your cash flow problems would go away.

The telephone:

I *hate* getting telemarketing calls.

No sooner have I sat down for supper than the phone rings. I answer, "Hello, Craig speaking", and then there is this short silence followed by a voice saying, "Hello, may I speak to Mr. Craig Copland please". Something inside me dies a little bit and I know that my number has come up on the predictive dialler. Soon an enthusiastic young person is encouraging me to buy light bulbs, or add insurance to my credit card, or send some poor kids off to see the circus, or send a boatload of goodies off to starving children in Botswana, or wherever. I really, really can't stand telemarketing.

I *love* telemarketing.

It one of the few tools available to non-profit that can generate pots of net income in a short period of time with no significant exposure to a financial loss. If your organization has a large file of lapsed direct mail donors who used to have an average gift of $40 or more then you are sitting on a gold mine for an emergency phone campaign.

Why?

Because neither Americans nor Canadians read anymore. It's not that we can't, it's just that we don't. But we always answer the telephone.

A WHYFU letter to a lapsed file may generate a response of three to four percent. At $1.25 cost per unit (including creative, postage, production, processing, depositing and data management) and an average gift of $30 you need a response of four percent just to break even. And you have to pay all your costs up front before you know whether or not you are going to make a nickel out of it or if you're going to lose thousands of dollars.

A well-run *phone* campaign usually secures a gift from twenty to twenty-five percent of a lapsed file. It costs about $4 per contact. Do the math. With an average gift of $30 and paid rate of twenty-five percent you are earning $3.50 net on every name on your list. Okay, so the overhead cost is well over fifty percent. Using the mail it's one hundred percent or more. And the exposure using the phone is minimal. If you aren't securing the sales rate you need after a few hours after a few hours of calling then you shut down the campaign and cap your loss at a minimum.

Long term it's always better to use direct mail to secure gifts from donors who have demonstrated that they are willing to respond to the mail. The cost per dollar received on a typical house mailing should be between fifteen to thirty percent depending on the response rate and average gift.

The cost of contacting the same list by phone will vary from forty to sixty percent depending on the same factors. But the <u>total net income</u> from a phone campaign will invariably be higher than from mailing to the same list because so many more donors will make donations.

So if you are in a bind, try this: mail an emergency appeal to your current donors. Those that do not respond after three weeks, phone. This will provide a short term spike to your cash flow, but that may be exactly what you need today to get over your crisis. You *will* have complaints. But we're talking tough times, short term. You can live with it. It doesn't have to last forever.

What can you sell or lease out?

Do you own late model vehicles? Sell them and lease replacements. Bad over the long run, but a source of cash today.

Your donor list? If it's big enough and clean enough then there are numerous direct marketing agencies who will pay cash for it. Or it could be rented out again and again at ten to fifteen cents a name. If you have privacy restrictions or have pledged to your donors that you wold not do this, then don't. But otherwise, think about it.

Can you squeeze your operation into less room, freeing up warehouse, commercial or retail space and putting it on the market? Do you have a field director in Indonesia who knows the country inside out and speaks the language? Let him or her serve as consultant to a Canadian mining company for three months. Sure, you're not going to like doing this. Some medicine has a bad taste. But if it will generate surplus cash quickly and allow you to keep your doors open, it's good for you.

Businesses in serious trouble sell their receivables to firms that specialize in collecting. Do you have pledges on record which were never paid or are way overdue? Maybe there's a firm who will buy them either for a percentage of their face value or on an income split.

Never thought of that one, did you?

Do you have services you can sell? Could you agree to provide donation caging and donor database management services for another non-profit around the corner for a reasonable fee?

Okay, maybe there are some things which you absolutely cannot do and you would rather have the organization die before doing them. Before you make that decision ask yourself if the child you're feeding in Haiti, or the welfare mom you're helping in Detroit, or the person dying from the disease you're helping to treat and prevent would share your convictions. If you're sure they would, fine. Fold. But if not, then hold your nose and swallow the medicine.

If you're about to go down almost nothing is sacred. Find cash and then think of more ways to find cash.

Cry wolf!

If the wolf is at the door then there is nothing wrong with letting people know. In fact, it's kind of dumb to keep it hush hush. Our refusal to let our world know we're in trouble usually has a lot more to do with our pride.

Get over it.

Shouting "Help!" now is a lot less embarrassing than saying "Sorry" later when they come to lock you out. So send out a desperate letter to all of your donors. Tell them the truth. Unless you get in a lot of money quickly you really may go out of business. Will some of them complain? Sure, wouldn't you? But more often than not they will respond and give you one of the highest rates of return and highest average gift rates to any direct mail appeal you have ever done.

Obviously you can't do this very often or you really would be just crying wolf. But an emergency appeal, followed a couple of months later by a "Thank you so much, but we're not quite out of the woods yet. Can you please give again?" does work. The response rate will be even better if you can do it over the phone instead of the mail. That type of campaign will really get people ticked off, but it works. You will lose a few supporters. You will make a lot of humble apologies. But you will get a lot of cash in quickly. Be open and tell people what happened and tell them about your plan for rebuilding.

Beg:

Have somebody from your non-profit meet personally with your major donors and ask for a special one-time emergency donation. Go to whatever branch of government that has provided funding for you in the past and work with their officers to see if there might be some money somewhere they could allocate to you. Most government officers who relate to non-profits are usually decent sorts who really do not want to see you go down, who know about all kinds of special funds floating around their department, and who may be very willing to work hard, even overtime, to help you pull things out of the fire.

Ask. Plead. Weep if necessary. If you think that major gifts or grants from individuals, corporations, foundations, or government funding offices are always made only according to objective criteria and that emotional responses have nothing to do with it, think again. People help people in need. People help people they like. People like lending a hand in a crisis. This will work. Once. Maybe twice if you go back and show how you have used their gift to save the organization, how your plan is working and how just one more gift will complete the turnaround. Don't even think about trying it three times. But don't let your pride hold you back from trying it once.

Make a Plan and put it on paper:

List all those things you are going to do to cut costs. And then all those things which will boost short-term cash flow. Assign specific dates for every action. Create a cash flow spreadsheet showing how you are going to stop going farther into the hole, turnaround, and get out. Take it out for two years, showing how you will re-invest a portion of your net income into long term fundraising programs that pay off more slowly, but at a lower overhead cost. Print the list, time line, and spreadsheet. Keep it simple.

Form a Turnaround Management Team:

The team should include your CEO, your board treasurer and/or chair, your CFO, maybe your director of development (unless he/she is one of the reasons for your predicament), your bank manager, a representative of your staff, and your major creditor (if applicable).

This group needs to meet once a week for an hour. I suggest every Tuesday morning, since by that time you should have the results from the previous week that were compiled every Monday. Make sure you have accurate and timely numbers every week for them to review.

This group is entrusted with the job of monitoring the implementation of the Turnaround Plan, revising it if some aspect isn't working and making sure that the steps to be taken are taken on time, and that the numbers projected for reduced costs and increased cash flow are hit.

The *No B.S.* board meeting:

If there is one thing that boards like less than bad news, its *surprise* bad news. If you are in a crisis then you need to tell your board chair that things are going badly, that a special board meeting needs to be called, and the unvarnished facts presented. It really helps if the Turnaround Plan is presented and shows a clear path of cost cutting and income producing activities that will lead the organization out of the financial wilderness. If the board is serious about turning the organization around then it will: 1. Lead by example and make significant and continuing cash contributions; 2. Set up meetings with prospective major individual or corporate donors and attend them; 3. Approve the cost cuts and income generators and suggest more of the same; 4. Select a crisis management team and empower it to act forcefully to implement the Plan.

The *No B.S.* creditor meetings:

Fortunately most non-profits facing a financial crisis have a very limited number of major creditors. These usually include their bank if a line of credit has been extended, individuals who hold notes on loans or bonds, direct mail firms, landlords, maybe a couple of other service providers, and possibly employees if you have deferred payment of wages. No creditor ever wants to put a non-profit out of business and almost every creditor would prefer to wait a few months longer and get paid all or almost all of what is owed than to force a non-profit into receivership and end up getting paid next to nothing. Other than the bank most creditors are unsecured and even those that are will come in behind the bank and so have little expectation of getting more than a few cents on the dollar.

So, go individually to each creditor and give them the choice. You say, "You can push us into receivership if you really want to. But here is the full disclosure of our assets and other creditors, so you won't get much, if anything. However, here is our Turnaround Plan which shows how we are moving to make a full financial recovery and here is our schedule of payments on your account. We are asking our creditors to appoint a representative on our Turnaround Management Team. And, of course, here is the donation amount which we would like you to write off from the amount we owe you to assist us in this process." Assuming they say yes to the Hobson's choice you present to them, you then send them a weekly memo from the Turnaround Management Team reviewing your progress, and you do everything possible to meet the schedule of payments on their account.

Merge:

In the private sector boards of directors are required by law to act in the interest of the shareholders of the corporation. If it in their interest to merge their company with another, or to allow their shares to be purchased and their company to be taken over, or to take over another corporation, they have to do it.

Non-profits boards and executives are under no such legal obligation, even if they should be under a moral one.

For example:

The United Kingdom has a population of about sixty million and about sixty non-profit organizations involved in some form of international aid. Canada has a population of about thirty million and about three hundred organizations involved in some form of international aid.

Canada has ten times too many.

Almost all Canadian aid agencies are offering some version of "Give a man a fish.............." or "Most important of all, you will give them HOPE!" There is really not a lot of difference in the policies or programs of many of these agencies to explain why there are so many of them.

Many Canadian aid agencies today are struggling financially because of the recession, because CIDA grants have been cut back, and because Canadians' interest in overseas relief and development has waned. But few are seriously considering a merger with other similar agencies.

Most of these charities appear to be willing to shrink to a fraction of their former size and emphasize their perceived distinctive character rather than merge with or be taken over by another agency. There is an element of preferring to be the "Big frog in a small puddle" mentality in some of their board members and staff. Again, this is one of those situations where if beneficiaries were shareholders, the mergers or takeovers would have happened long ago.

If the prospects for a financial turnaround are bleak, or even if your beneficiaries would receive significantly more benefit from the cost-efficiency of merged organizations, then this is a direction you need to consider.

Share the challenge, share the credit:

Cutting costs is always painful, especially if it involves terminations. But once the Turnaround Plan for cost cutting and income generation is agreed upon, implement the cuts as quickly as possible.

If you had to let a number of staff go then those remaining behind will most certainly be in shock and demoralized, assuming that their days are numbered as well. So call together the remaining staff with selected members of the board present. Present to them the hard facts of the situation being faced as well as the Turnaround Plan. Answer all of their questions. Ask for and listen to some of their suggestions for cutting more costs and generating cash flow.

Do not minimize the seriousness of the current situation. Note the board members' leadership in giving time and donations. Ask staff openly and candidly for their support and the additional effort *above and beyond*. Present the challenge and ask them to share in it with you. Ask them to appoint a representative to the Turnaround Management Team.

Then continue to meet with the staff on a weekly or fortnightly basis and bring them up to date. As numbers start to turn around give credit and praise to those employees who have had a hand in making it happen. Give rewards in the form of personal thank you notes from the board chair or other forms of recognition.

Use the passing of certain milestones in the Turnaround Plan as an excuse to celebrate. Have the board members cover the costs of a pizza and soft drink lunch where results are announced to staff. If you have leftover T-shirts, or mugs, or whatever in the store room give each of the staff something.

If you are a board member or executive officer please do not try to focus credit for turnaround achievements on yourself, even if you know in your heart of hearts that *you* played a major role in making things happen. Give the credit to others, especially the rank and file employees. Thank them for what they have done not only to save the organization but also to preserve the service to your beneficiaries.

And don't mess up again:

Once organizations start to see improved cash flow one of the first things I see them doing is starting to hire more staff. Wrong thing to do. When almost everybody is complaining that they need more help, and your debts are paid off, and you are contributing to your reserve fund, and your cash flow is permitting increased contributions to your beneficiaries, perhaps then you could consider increasing your payroll. And even then ask employees if they could wait maybe three or six more months. There will be pressure to add others costs as well. But you will have proven that you can operate much leaner than before. Don't let the fat creep back in.

.

Part Two

How to do Fundraising that Brings in Cash Now

There are hundreds of books available on fundraising. Some are highly sophisticated and cover things like estate planning, revocable and non-revocable trusts, corporate social responsibility, and so on. These are all good things for successful major non-profits to do.

But if you are a struggling organization that has just recently gone through a cash flow crisis and almost had to close your doors then you don't have the leisure to pursue long-range strategies today. Maybe tomorrow.

Today you have to focus on those fundraising activities that will return net income this week, this quarter, this year.

The pages that follow tell you how to do that. All of the instructions are directed towards fundraising actions that have an immediate or almost immediate return. If you do not already have programs like these in place, get them there. If you do have them, then do whatever is necessary to make them more effective.

Chapter Six – Monthly Giving

I have chosen to start with what I have had to acknowledge is the best overall long-term method for raising funds for non-profit organizations – getting your supporters to agree to give a regular amount every month using pre-authorized contributions from their credit cards or bank accounts.

Why?

Most of you who are reading this will at one time or other have sponsored a child through World Vision, Christian Children's Fund, Feed the Children, Plan, or one of the other humanitarian aid organizations that you see night after night running TV infomercials and asking you to make a difference in the life of a child.

Why do they do it? Why do they promote monthly donations that are directly connected to an individual child?

Because it works.

Child sponsorship is by far the most effective fundraising method that has ever been developed for securing donations from individuals for causes related to foreign aid. It has been criticized (by those organizations that do not use it) as being patronizing, or having high administrative overheads, or failing to address the real causes of poverty, but the fact remains that more than half of all donations given by Americans and Canadians to alleviate third world poverty is given through child sponsorship.

And frankly, it makes sense. Do the math.

The average family, especially in times of economic recession, is not likely to write a check for $360 for an appeal for third world poverty. But there are very few individuals or families who perceive that their situation is so dire that they cannot spare "just one dollar a day" knowing that a small daily amount like that is all it takes to change the life of a child.

If child sponsors elect to send in a check every month for $30 then the rate of missed or forgotten payments and the drop off rate is high. However, once they authorize an organization to take $30 a month off of their credit card then the donation becomes automatic, and the rate of missed payments and cancellations diminishes incredibly. The donor has to initiate an action to *not* send in a gift every month. A few will, but for the rest of us the donation line on our credit card statement is small change compared to everything else that appears there and, sadly, often less than the monthly interest that we end up paying.

Child sponsorship is also the most *cost effective* means of raising funds from average American families. The overhead cost of acquiring a monthly sponsor may be higher than getting someone to make a first time one-off donation, but the standard child sponsor stays with the program for an average of seven years, during which time the cost of raising each dollar given continues to fall. Over time the fundraising cost incurred by most of the larger and very responsible child sponsorship agencies falls to around twenty to twenty-five cents on the dollar. In today's market place that is far better that you can achieve from direct mail, telemarketing, or even email appeals.

It order to keep monthly sponsors engaged an organization must keep in contact with the sponsor and send him or her regular updates on the well-being of the child. If this is done faithfully then the donor forms an emotional bond with the child and often with the staff who communicate on behalf of the child.

When a crisis does come along, such as an earthquake in Haiti, those individuals who are already giving every month will be among the most likely to contribute over and above to an organization that they have come to know and trust.

All of the above applies to all other non-profit organizations as well.

The average family today is not likely to perceive themselves to be in a position to cut a personal check for $1,800 as a contribution to your organization. But could they be persuaded that they could sacrifice the equivalent of a daily visit to *Starbucks* – five dollars a day; more if you're into *soy chai lattes?*

Sure, it's the same in the long run but it *seems* like a lot less.

If five dollars a day is too steep for your supporters then start off at a lower rate – two dollars a day. Even one dollar a day. Over time you can encourage many of them to upgrade to a higher daily level.

If appealed to effectively, many monthly sponsors to non-profits can be encouraged to continue to make a monthly donation even after the particular issue they agreed to help support has been accomplished.

The cost of acquiring a new donor by direct mail or telephone is usually one hundred percent or more of the first donation (more on this below when we get to those methods). Usually twenty-five to forty percent of those who make a first donation to the phone or through the mail do not go on to make a second or subsequent donation, having done their part by giving once. Making subsequent appeals to them by phone or mail will cost from twenty percent to fifty percent of what is received from those donations. By comparison, the cost of acquiring a new monthly sponsor may be up to three hundred percent of their first donation, but the overhead cost of subsequent donations usually hovers around three to five percent of what is received. Over the life of a campaign, and often beyond, the overall overhead cost of pre-authorized monthly income continues to fall.

The point of all of this?

Do everything you can to encourage your supporters to give every month. Do whatever it takes to get your occasional mail, phone, Internet, or event donors to sign up to monthly giving. Keep them engaged by sending regular personalized newsletters and emails. Send special invitations to events and opportunities to meet your leaders. Phone them occasionally not to ask for more money but just to thank them. Send them occasional premiums, small token gifts, signed photos, or other modest items as a way of showing them your appreciation. Acknowledge them on your list of donors on your website. Make them feel appreciated.

Do all of the above and your faithful monthly donors will stay with you for years, providing you with a generous and reliable cash flow at very little overhead cost.

The first choice for a method of developing a monthly giving program is one in which one hundred percent of the income comes directly to the organization. If you consistently ask your donors to become pre-authorized monthly supporters then you should be able to upgrade five to ten percent of them to that level.

Once you have done that then you will need some additional incentive to convince them to make a monthly contribution. Below is a way of doing that by offering back to your donors the right to membership in a buyers' club that gives them hundreds of dollars in discounts on consumer goods and services.

A Recommended Method of Building a Monthly Giving Program

(Alert: the author has a pecuniary interest in this program. Check it out at **www.donorclub.org**. Contact me at **craig@donorclub.org** or call me at (202) 621-0601 to arrange to test it for your organization.)

Donor Club.org

What is it?

It's a buyers' club designed for individuals and families who give to non-profit organizations. It's a way of expressing thanks to these donors of AND as a way of upgrading occasional donors to monthly giving. Your donors are invited to join a buyers' club through which they will be able to save hundreds of dollars off the cost of necessary everyday consumer items, travel, and insurance products. Those who join the Club pay monthly membership fees. Fifty percent of their fees go directly to the organization with which they are connected.

What's in it for the participating non-profit organization?

Substantial reliable pre-authorized monthly income; no fundraising overhead cost; appreciation and rewards to donors and members; significant savings in everyday purchases and travel costs to your donors and members; an opportunity to test and try the program with no obligation.

How can the organizations control what is being communicated to their donors or members?

Participating organizations have final sign-off on all printed materials and telephone scripts. Nothing can be communicated without their full approval. Any phone calls placed would be fully recorded and available for review.

What does it cost the participating organizations?

The fundraising component is **free**. All of the sales and marketing expenses are paid by DonorClub. The administration and management of the members' accounts are also fully covered by DonorClub. Participating organizations are expected only to communicate with those who join and welcome them to the Club. These monthly donors should then receive standard newsletters and other types of communication from the non-profit in order to keep them informed and motivated to continue to support the non-profit and its cause.

How will the non-profit's donors or members be contacted?

Several ways. Inserts can be placed in mailings sent to donors or members. These can either be front end lift premiums inviting donors who make a donation to join the Club, or a back end premium inserted into a receipt or thank-you mailing. Inserts and ads could also be placed in an organization's newsletters. The program could be featured on their websites. Pitches to sign up could also be made at any of an organization's events. Occasional phone calls could be placed to donors thanking them for their support, and offering club membership as a way of showing appreciation. If the organization regularly sends out email communication then the DonorClub offer could be attached to those emails.

How can we know for sure that we are receiving the full amount owed to us?

DonorClub will issue a complete print out every month to back up the 50% revenue share. If the organization wishes to review DonorClub's records or have them reviewed by the organization's auditor, this can be arranged. Alternatively, DonorCub's merchant bank that processes the members' credit card payments will split the deposit and send the 50% directly to the organization's bank account without those funds ever entering the DonorClub's accounts. The organization, however, would be responsible for the related bank charges for this service.

Can any organization participate?

You should have a donor/member base of 5000 people or more. Smaller organizations could pool their members. Participation is open to any *bona fide* non-profit organization.

Can the donor claim a tax credit for the donation portion of the fee?

No. Even if the organization is a registered Canadian charity or a US 501 (c) (3) it is our understanding that the neither the CRA nor the IRS look kindly on claiming a tax credit for a donation that was given with a clearly understood expectation of a monetary return to the donor. In this case the resulting monetary benefit to the donor would be worth several times the value of the actual donation so no receipt should be issued. Participating organizations need to confirm this with their own legal counsel, and the IRS or CRA.

What if we don't have enough staff or time to handle questions or concerns our donors might have that arise from buyers' club aspect of this program?

That's okay. We do. We don't want you to have to handle questions from your donors or members. We want to handle them. DonorClub has a customer service number that is available and manned constantly. Members are given that number and encouraged to call in to ask about anything. If anybody calls your organization, just forward the call to our center.

Who is behind this?

DonorClub.org© is a program owned by Continuity Partners Inc., a division of Avalon Marketing Group of Nevada, Montreal, Canada and the UK. They have been operating buyers' clubs for over a decade. Conservative Growth Inc., of Washington DC and Toronto, is a marketing agent for their programs. The concept has been developed as a "private sector / non-profit sector partnership."

Is there any advantage to being an early adapter?

Yes. In addition to the obvious benefit of starting immediately to receive monthly net income with no fundraising cost, there is also the advantage of being the first organization to enroll an individual member or donor. Over the next few months this program will be offered to non-profits throughout the US and Canada. Many prospective members of the Club will donate to numerous organizations over the course of a couple of years. However, they will only join the DonorClub program once, and that will be through the first group that invites them. It will be that organization that will receive the monthly allocation of their fee.

How can we use this to cultivate brand loyalty to our organization and campaign?

We offer the option of "White Labeling" the program so that it would be presented as "The XYZ Foundation Donor Club." If you wish, the listing on the member's credit card statement can give your organization's name.

If this program would be useful to your turnaround campaign program, please contact me at **Craig@DonorClub.org** *or call (202) 621-0601.*

Chapter Seven - Person to Person Fundraising

There have been great advances in the past ten years in various methods of automated fundraising and fundraising contracted out to third-party experts. However, face-to-face personal fundraising is still a highly effective way to secure major contributions from wealthier donors. When you are trying to work your way out of a financial crisis, it is essential.

Face-to-face personal fundraising is the most time consuming way to raise money and takes the greatest preparation. *But it is absolutely worth it.*

Many corporations and individuals with high net worth give nothing to non-profits. When asked why they don't, by far the most common reply is *"nobody asked me."* For these people and companies, getting a letter or a phone call does not constitute being asked. It has to be personal.

How to do face-to-face fundraising

Preparation:

The first person to contribute to a turnaround campaign should be the founder or current leader of the organization. These people have to "put their money where their mouth is" and be seen to be doing so. Their contribution should be appropriate to their means.

The second group of donors to a turnaround campaign should be the founder's or CEO's family members, extended family, personal friends, and business colleagues. If those who know the organization and its leader best aren't willing to give their financial support, it sends a very loud message to other potential donors.

The initial ask made to the above people should be made directly by the organization's leader before he or she even announces the campaign.

The fundraising team then starts by identifying all possible prospects for major gifts.

These include:

Family and friends. Board members and senior staff have to identify those closest to them and ask for their help on the behalf of the campaign, and if they already have been asked, then ask them again, and again.

Friends and associates through church/synagogue, neighbors, business connections, service clubs, fraternal organizations, PTA, etc.

Friends and associates of the members of the fundraising staff and volunteers and the Turnaround Team from the same groups.

All former donors to previous campaigns.

Leaders and known contact people within supportive corporations, homeowners groups, chambers of commerce, professional organizations, churches and synagogues, women's groups, . . . and everyone else you can think of who is likely to support your cause.

Next: the Team and staff reviews the list of prospects and assigns to each of the names: a) the amount they realistically think might be given; b) the name of the person within the team who has the best personal contact with the prospect; and c) the specific issues related to the campaign and the cause that the prospect is most likely to feel strongly about.

Then: someone calls the prospect – ideally the person with the closest personal connection – and asks for a twenty-minute appointment sometime within the coming two weeks to talk to them about the campaign and how they might be able to help. If the prospect agrees and a time is set, then the conversation ends courteously and an immediate email is sent thanking the prospect for agreeing to meet and confirming the time and place.

If a prospect agrees to meet, then you can be quite certain that he or she knows why you are asking for a meeting and is more than likely prepared to make some sort of contribution.

The more senior the prospect and the more you plan to ask him or her for, the more senior the delegates that go to the meeting on behalf of the campaign.

The CEO or campaign leader should participate in every meeting with those who are expected to be the top twenty-five percent of major donors. The individual that had the connection and made the call to ask for the appointment should also attend.

There should be no more than three people in a delegation unless you are meeting with the executive members of an organization. Never overwhelm the prospect with the size of your delegation.

Some experienced CEO's or board members can manage these

meetings all by themselves. But it is usually more comfortable to use a tag team approach and send at least one other person to help out.

Those going to the meeting need to meet at least fifteen minutes beforehand to review their notes and preparation and roles in the meeting.

Be on time. Dress appropriately.

At the meeting:

Accept coffee or water. Turn down food or booze.

The contact person greets the prospect and, if necessary, introduces the organization's CEO and whoever else has come along.

Chit chat to break the ice for two to three minutes (weather, local sports, current news item, family members, etc.). Do not engage in intense conversation about issues related to the turnaround campaign.

The designated introductory speaker brings the conversation to the reason for the meeting – the cause of the organization and the campaign.

Do not hand the prospect a folder or brochure at this point. It will only distract from the conversation. Such items are "leave behinds."

A simple, reliable approach is to have prepared four pages of paper. Each team member has one set, with enough other sets for the prospect(s) and a couple of extras in case the prospect has invited others to the meeting.

Each page has a heading and four or five bullet points.

Hand the pages to the potential donor *one at a time* and read and comment on them *briefly*.

For example . . .

If your non-profit organization provides services to children and youth in your community and is in financial crisis because of the cuts in government funding then you could use a four-step approach as follows:

First page: *The needs facing children and youth in our community*

A brief list of the three or four major challenges faced by the children and youth your organization serves, and the names of the excellent programs you operate to help them. The list should be customized so that the major concerns of the potential donor are included.

Second page: *The crisis – why your organization is in trouble and the impending closure of your doors if a solution cannot be found.*

A few bullet points noting what happened and the consequences.

Third page: *The Turnaround Plan*

A five or six-point summary of your plan for recovery and moving forward; the steps approved by the board that are being taken to respond to the crisis so that the children and youth who need you will continue to be served.

Fourth page: *The Turnaround Finance Plan*

A list of your planned fund-raising activities showing projected income, for example, from your planned gala, house parties, major corporate donations, direct mail, telemarketing, Internet blasts, and personal contributions from board members and major donors.

The final point reads something like: "Our plan includes a major donation from John Smith (the person you are talking to) of $2000 a month from now until the end of the calendar year."

This final section should be personally customized for each

individual, small corporation, major corporation, or organization you are meeting with and be appropriate to past donations and perceived capacity to support you.

Then, look directly at the potential donor and say (something like), "John, would you be willing to help us to respond to this crisis so that we can continue to help our community's children. Could you do so by donating $2000 a month for the next twelve months?"

Then *stop talking* and wait for an answer. *Do not keep talking and do not ever water down the request if the donor looks like he or she is uncomfortable with the amount you have suggested.*

Sometimes it may be appropriate if a friend or colleague of the donor is present to do the ask by saying something like, "My wife Amanda and I have agreed to give $2000 a month to help this project, and we were hoping that you and Sue could join us with a matching amount. Would you be okay with a commitment like that?" (or words to that effect). *But then stop talking and let the donor respond.*

If the donor responds with something like, "Well I'd like to help out, but the amount you're suggesting is a little rich for us," then say something like, "Well, what amount would you be comfortable with?" *And then be quiet and let him or her respond.*

Personal face-to-face fundraising takes planning, time, and emotional energy. It's hard to sit in front of people and ask for money. But if someone has agreed to meet, then it is highly likely that they know why you are there, that they support your cause, and are interested in helping. Just do it.

Schedule one to three meetings a week. Every week. Start early. Never stop.

How to do personal fundraising on the phone:

Both the percentage of prospects who say "yes" and the average gift will be lower in response to a phone conversation than when meeting face-to-face, but you can talk to many more people in an hour over the phone than face-to-face.

Very few CEO's, board members, or senior staff like "dialing for dollars." Most hate it. Many will come up with every excuse in the book to find something else to do. Don't let that happen. You have to make the calls.

It works. Forty to fifty percent of individuals contacted personally over the phone by someone they know and respect will agree to make a donation. Most will make a much higher donation than they would in response to a direct mail or commercial telemarketing appeal.

Use the right caller. The best results will be achieved from calls placed by the organization's founder or CEO. The next best are the founder's spouse or family member if they are comfortable with doing so, followed by a board member, senior staff person, or senior volunteer member.

Use the right list. Start with a list of all those who gave to previous campaigns in response to a personal phone call. Build the list by adding every family member, personal friend, fellow church member, business associate, fellow club member, and neighbor of the CEO or board members.

Do not waste the valuable time of the CEO or a senior volunteer caller by having them call names out of the phone book or a list that has not been updated in the past year.

Use a script so that the conversation stays on topic. Make sure that the caller has the script memorized *but* has practiced delivering it enough times so that it sounds natural and casual.

The caller needs to have either a cue card or a digital screen in front of him or her while making the call. The card/screen must have the proper first and last names of the potential donor being called as well as names of other family members, especially the spouse if that information is available. The card should, if at all possible, also have some basic information about the donor such as his or her previous donations and to what project they were made, along with any pertinent information about his or her vocation, profession, church or community organization, or other link to your organization or cause.

The script begins with a request to speak to the potential donor. Ask for him or her by first name. Once you have confirmed that the person you are trying to reach is on the phone, you clearly identify yourself by name as the senior staff member or volunteer board member calling on behalf of the campaign.

The opening two or three lines are critical. You must engage the donor's emotions by noting some of the issues that community members care deeply about in your local area and that are directly connected to your cause. Then explain the crisis *briefly* and move immediately to the steps being taken to make sure that the organization can continue to serve the community.

Then ask the donor for an amount appropriate to his or her past donations.

Then be quiet and wait for the donor to answer. If they seem interested but are balking at the amount suggested, either slide to a somewhat lower amount or ask them to state an amount that they would be comfortable with.

If at all possible, have them give you their credit card information so that the gift can be put to work right away. If they will not offer the credit card details, then reconfirm their current mailing address. Thank them and move on to the next call.

Make sure that if they pledged a donation but did not give it on credit card that a pledge collection note is sent out *immediately*, including a stamped return envelope.

If they did give the donation by credit card, then make sure that a thank-you note signed by the CEO or board member is sent out immediately.

Like it or not, the most effective time to reach people at home is over the supper hour. If calling at that time, always begin with a sincere but brief apology for disturbing their dinner hour and then start the conversation. The most effective time to reach people at the place of work is between 8:00 am and 9:30 am.

When ending up in voice mail, leave a brief friendly message about who is calling and why, and state that you will call again the next day, or within a few days. And then do it.

The greatest enemy of telephone fundraising is Caller ID. If people see an 800-number, or "Unknown Caller" or "Blocked" message, they are far less likely to answer the call. This applies to both personal calls and commercial calls made from a call center. Make sure that the caller ID shows up as the personal name of the caller or the organization.

Record: 1) all donations made over the phone; 2) those who pledged and were sent a collection note in the mail; 3) the donations received with the dates and amounts given; 4) the name of the person who made the call. This information will be very valuable for future campaigns. All this information should go into your donor database.

If a pledged donation has not been received within three weeks of its having been made, send out a reminder note. If it still does not come in after another three weeks, send another reminder note. After that, write it off and note in the records that the person called made a pledge but did not fulfill. Next time around don't bother calling that person.

Dialing for dollars is a necessary part of non-profit life. Many non-profit CEO's and directors of development set aside time every day or at least every week to call their major donors, bring them up to date on what is happening with respect to the cause and the organization and ask again for their financial support. If you are going to be in philanthropic life then you may as well get used to it, and get good at it. If it had been a consistent part of how you operated in the past you would not be in financial crisis now.

Chapter Eight - Events

How to Raise Funds at Large-Scale Events

Large-scale events such as galas, banquets, concerts, and rallies have the potential to raise a lot of money in a short period of time and be a great source of energy and momentum for an organization's campaign.

They are wonderful ways of introducing potential donors and volunteers to the cause and of persuading those new to your organization to support you.

One single highly successful large-scale event has the potential to make your financial crisis vanish all by itself.

Large events also have the potential to lose a lot of money very quickly. They can go badly. They always seem to cost more than planned. So it is really important to follow the guidelines given below.

Finances and planning:

Start planning a long way ahead – at least three months.

Put together a small team of volunteers, assisted by a staff member, as the event planning committee. It's very important that at least a couple of these people have had previous event planning experience.

Set goals for attendees, gross and net income, new donors, and VIP's attending.

If money permits, hire an event planner.

Secure all necessary items in advance, in writing – the venue rental, the printing, the catering, the paid media, the talent, the MC.

If planning a large outdoor event, always have a Plan B in case of bad weather.

It's always better to have a venue that is a bit too crowded than one that is too large for the number of people who attend and that feels empty.

If you are selling tickets it is imperative that you have a network of volunteer sellers who in turn have an extensive network of friends and contacts to sell tickets to. Most people buy tickets from other people who invite them to join them. Very few buy in response to a poster or an email.

Do not rely on paid media, posters, or mailings to sell tickets.

Try to never pay for anything. Always ask to have it donated, or at least partially donated.

Never run an open bar unless you have extensive insurance, and a good lawyer.

Get sponsors. Give them a good opportunity to promote themselves.

If possible, include a silent or live auction, raffle, and memento sales as part of the event. Have several ticket sellers schmoozing among the crowd selling raffle tickets.

Always try to have all of the costs fully covered by sponsorships. Income from ticket sales, auctions, raffles and donations should be 100 percent profit. Never count on ticket sales to cover a shortfall in income necessary to pay for expenses.

It's also imperative that costs be tightly controlled. Require budgets from all members of the team for their areas of responsibility. Tightly limit those permitted to spend money.

Be very cautious of last minute panic spending. "In for a dime, in for a dollar" can kill.

Set aside a specific time in the program when someone addresses the crowd and effectively asks them for donations, using the forms and envelopes distributed to everyone. Make sure that people can give by credit card as well as with checks or cash.

The program:

People consider events to be successful if they enjoy them. People enjoy events where they chat with friends, make new friends, and get a chance to speak even briefly with the CEO, organization founder, supporting celebrity, or at least his or her family members or senior staff people, especially if they have a few really hearty laughs while talking with people they like and admire.

Keep the program tight and moving. Have an experienced MC who can call the room to order, forcefully but pleasantly, and introduce the various participants.

Acknowledge and thank the sponsors and visiting dignitaries generously. Unless unavoidable or completely inappropriate, do not ask any of them to speak. They always go on too long.

Lead-up items on the program, including entertainment, should be few and short. Be careful about letting these items go on for more than thirty minutes.

Testimonials from ordinary folk are very important. If you are doing something for troubled youth then have one or two of the successful graduates of your program speak briefly about his or her life and the positive impact your programs made. If you are helping overseas then have someone who has actually been to the project talk about his or her experience briefly.

PowerPoint and audio/visual presentations should only supplement the program not *be* the program. They need to be relatively short. People give to people, not to PowerPoint.

Do not introduce the wonderful person, who will introduce the wonderful person, who will introduce the local dignitary, who will introduce the speaker. One introduction is all you need. Keep it short. Nobody should outshine or upstage the speaker.

If the speaker is the CEO then he or she might also make the appeal for financial support. If the speaker is a celebrity or dignitary, then the person who thanks the speaker should also then give the pitch for campaign donations. This person should be one having stature and respect in the community. He or she might also give a brief testimonial confirming that they or their family have made a major financial commitment to the campaign and are asking the rest of the room to join them in supporting the organization, help children in need . . . whatever.

Mementos and party favors should be neither extravagant nor immediately disposable. T-shirts are affordable and also serve to promote the organization if they look good enough to be worn later.

It's imperative that all attendees and especially donors and sponsors receive a personal thank-you note within a few days after the event.

Also imperative is that the contact information for all attendees be secured and entered into your database. Everyone should be contacted within two to three weeks, given a brief update on the campaign, and asked for a subsequent donation.

Food:

It is easier to have a reception with finger food instead of a sit-down banquet, and it's a lot less expensive. If serving sit-down food, make helpings generous but not extravagant. Healthy food is in.

Make sure the venue can deliver a good hot dinner to the size of crowd you expect to have. Get references beforehand and get all menu items specified in writing.

Careful with the booze. While some of us of a certain age bemoan the demise of the serious cocktail party and the miserable substitution of white wine for good gin, it is better to go the wine route if you are serving alcohol at all. Placing one bottle of red and one of white on the table is a common practice, as is having the servers come around and pour a glass at a time. Never let anyone leave drunk.

Try to get a corporate donor to sponsor a portion of the banquet.

Themed events:

Flea markets, car washes, art sales, barbeques, concerts, battle of the bands, sporting events, book readings and signings, costume parties, historical costumes, and other activities can work well for fundraising.

Innovative events can be effective and fun and may attract media. But be sure to sound them out with a number of people before undertaking. They can also bomb.

Golf tournaments, if properly planned and run, can be highly effective, especially if the founder, CEO or board chair are also enthusiastic golfers and participants. There is no apparent limit to how much money golf nuts will part with. An experienced team to plan and run the tournament is essential.

Third-party events:

Events run by other organizations with the net proceeds for your campaign are almost always a good thing. You just show up, have a good time, and pick up the check.

Some caution is required concerning donations you receive from groups that may not be appropriate to your platform or helpful to your reputation.

Do full research on any group that wants to sponsor an event but that is new to your organization.

A member of the fundraising staff needs to work alongside the group, especially if it has not helped you in the past, just to make sure that no blunders are made that could negatively reflect on your organization.

With the above cautions in mind, go and ask appropriate third-party groups to host an event for you. Possible groups might include a veterans' organization, Chamber of Commerce, local business or business association, church, non-profit organization, sport club, or professional association. Any groups that the CEO or board members have personally been associated with, or that has an affinity to your cause could be approached.

How to raise funds at small-scale events:

Invitation-only gatherings of ten to fifty people in private homes, church or synagogue halls, country or business clubs, galleries, or other more intimate venues are among the most effective ways of raising immediate cash with little risk of high costs.

Such events are an efficient way of meeting community leaders and those with sufficient means to make a major contribution. They also let these people see who else is there and supporting you. These events are very useful for letting the board members and development staff make a personal connection with many community leaders in a short period of time.

People of wealth and/or community leadership are not particularly attracted to rah-rah mass events. They are much more motivated by an opportunity to become part of an inner circle of people who know (or at least have met) the organization's CEO or founder personally and expressed their thoughts to him or her, even if only briefly. Small-scale events permit this in a way that large-scale ones do not.

Decide on the venue in consultation with the host. Spacious private homes are always a good choice as long as they are easy to get to and there is adequate parking available. Whenever possible, the host of the event will pick up the entire tab

The invitations should be sent personally by the event host, in consultation with the development staff. They should be sent about three weeks before the intended event. Include an RSVP, preferably with a smaller addressed return envelope.

Send two or three times as many invitations as the actual number expected to attend. The people you are inviting are busy people and although interested and supportive, they will often have conflicts in their schedule.

Invitations need to follow common-sense rules of including the date, time, location directions, dress, cost (if applicable), name of the party to whom checks should be made out, and instructions on sending in a contribution even if they cannot attend.

Again, careful on the booze. Best to have volunteers (students are great at this) bring around trays with glasses of wine, champagne, juice, water or soda. Do not set out an open wine table or liquor bar.

Do not provide seating for more than a few people who might

actually need it (elderly, heavy, pregnant, disabled). When too many people sit down, an event dies.

Get the names and contact information of everybody that attends. Send immediate thank-you notes to all of them, noting their generous donations.

Make sure that the CEO or special celebrity gets to meet and chat briefly with as many guests as possible. That's why they came. After thirty to forty-five minutes of schmoozing, a member of the staff or board calls the crowd to order. The host is thanked. Any important officials are recognized briefly. The speaker is introduced. The organization's CEO or designated speaker speaks for no more than twenty minutes.

Don't forget to ask for money. There are several ways. The main speaker can include an appeal in his or her address. The host can give a testimonial asking all the guests to join him or her in making a generous donation. Guests should have received donation forms and envelopes in advance of this moment.

A few weeks later call all those who donated and again thank them for their support and, if appropriate, ask for an additional contribution if they are in a position to afford to give more. Submit all bills to the treasurer and record everything, regardless of who paid for it.

Make it fun. Guests should leave not only having personally met and heard from the CEO or celebrity but also having shared conversations with old and new friends. Have several team members serve as incognito hosts or hostesses who are responsible for greeting and introducing people to each other, chatting and picking up anyone who appears to be standing alone.

Chapter Nine - Direct Mail

For over thirty years, direct mail has been the one of the most important means of promoting non-profit causes in America.

Every year it raises hundreds of millions of dollars for all sort of organizations.

Direct mail is still the second largest form of advertising (by dollars spent and sales generated) in the nation.

It not only raises a lot of money, it informs and educates the recipient, strengthens the knowledgeable convictions of your supporters, helps identify potential major donors and volunteers, and motivates your donors to get more involved with your organization and cause.

So . . . what's the problem?

Direct mail is no longer the goldmine it was twenty-five years ago. It's time-consuming to do properly. If done badly it may deliver no net income or even a serious financial loss.

So . . . do it, but do it well.

Many non-profit organizations use a direct mail consulting firm to manage their programs. These are usually a good investment. Ask around and find a well-recommended firm. Do not leave the writing and management of a mail program to well-intentioned volunteer amateurs.

There are lots of books all about direct mail. One of the best for non-profits is Ben Hart's *Fund Your Cause with Direct Mail*. I strongly recommend getting it and doing what it says.

If you do not already have a direct mail program in place, the middle of a financial crisis may not the time to start one. There is a risk of loss on prospect mailings, and even if the program performs well from the start it will take at least a year for it to deliver significant net income. If you already have a house list, then use it in the ways described in earlier parts of this book. If you don't then it may be better to wait until you are out of danger and then start to implement a program. However, if you are going to use direct mail then you need to follow the guidelines below.

The List – the most important factor:

It's imperative that you send the right letter to the right list of the right people. *Who* gets the letter will have a far greater impact on your results than the content or appearance of the letter, or name of the signer.

There are two major types of lists– *prospect* lists and *house* lists.

Prospect lists are names of people that have never before sent you a donation, but they generally fit the profile of someone who you think might be likely to support your cause (e.g. If you are an environmental non-profit then someone who subscribes to *National Geographic* is more likely to be sympathetic to your organization than someone who subscribes to *Forbes*. You get the idea).

House lists are the names of people that have already given at least one donation in the past. Simply put, a direct mail program begins with mailings to prospect lists in order to find new first-time donors. Once they have made a first donation they are added to your house list. Then you send them appeal letters on a regular basis and ask for their continuing support.

Prospecting:

Never just send letters out to names from the phone book. It's a sure way to go broke.

The best general source of prospect lists is from other non-profits who support causes that are similar to yours. Appeal to all of these like-minded organizations and ask to use trade lists. These will be the richest large prospect lists available to you. There are many list brokers and direct mail consultants that arrange list trading.

If your organization is locally focused then another good source of lists is from local organizations that are active in the community. Churches, chambers of commerce, business associations, Rotary and similar service or fraternal groups, golf and other sport clubs, and other local organizations may allow you to send a prospect mailing or two to their membership lists. Some will not, for privacy reasons. But it doesn't hurt to ask.

Never send letters out to an entire large list (10,000+) the first time.

Always do a small (1000–5000 pieces) mailing to any list as a market test.

Names should be randomly selected. You can test several lists at a time. You can also test several versions of the same prospect letter.

Always track results. You need to record the specific results for each prospect list and each version of the letter according to how many responses were received per day, the average gift, the percent of responses to the number of units sent out, the specific geographic regions from which the responses were received, and the number of undeliverable returns.

After about three weeks, you should be able to compare the results and know which list delivered the best rate of response, which the best average gift, and which version of the letter did best.

If your response rate to the names from any particular list is one percent or higher and the average gift is $25 or better, then that's likely a very good list to use again for a larger mailing, usually called a "roll out" prospect mailing.

If the response rate is .5 percent or lower and the average gift is $15 or less, then that list is likely not worth rolling out.

Today you will do well if your total income from a prospect mailing breaks even against your hard costs. Even if the cost of the prospect mailing is marginally more than your return, it may still be useful to roll out the prospect (as long as your cash position can absorb the temporary shortfall) since you will recover any small loss and make net income on subsequent house mailings to those who responded.

Lists that are tested for prospect mailings but that do not perform acceptably should be discarded.

Caution: A lot of money can be lost by sending a large prospect mailing to a list that was not tested. There are horror stories of organizations that lost $100,000 or more. Don't do it. Always, always test first.

Also, compare the various versions of the letter sent out. Decide which version gets the best results and stick with that version. It will become your *control piece*. As long as your cash position can absorb it, keep on testing and rolling out prospect mailings in order to acquire as many new donors as quickly as possible. Keep acquiring and testing different prospect lists of likely donors and rolling out those that have adequate results.

House lists:

Your "house list" is the list of all those who have made at least one donation to your organization in the past. This is the list from which you will generate net income to pay for program expenses.

Every organization should be sending at least one letter to this list every two months even when there is no special project or emergency campaign appeal.

You do this so your donors will keep you in mind and continue to feel a part of your organization. Do not forget that these same people are receiving several letters every week from other compelling and worthwhile causes. You don't want them to forget about you and transfer all their interest to other organizations.

It is imperative that you keep very close track of the response rates to every house mailing. You may wish to test various versions of each house mailing to determine what issues and what ways of asking work best for your donors.

For every house mailing you should compile a spreadsheet showing the date of mailing, the number of units mailed, the responses received each day, the average gift and any differences among different versions of the same letter.

It is also imperative that you keep track of the response of every individual donor on the house list. Larger and more sophisticated organizations will want to adapt each letter to each donor so that the donor receives the form of the letter that has been shown to elicit the greatest response. Smaller campaigns still need to review the response of each individual donor to be sure to catch those that have stopped giving and send them a special appeal designed for lapsed donors.

It is also imperative that the house list be kept clean. It is all too easy to end up with a donor database in which you have the same donor listed two or more times with minor differences in the name or address. The duplicates need to be removed regularly. Similarly, if a letter is returned because of a wrong address you need to take steps to either update and correct the address or remove the name from the current house file so that you will not be sending any more letters to the that address.

You also need to segment your list and extract your best donors from the so-so ones. Anyone who sends you $200 or more once, or cumulative donations of $300 within a year, should not be treated the same way as the rest of the list. These names should receive a more personalized, hand-signed letter and possibly be selected for a personal phone call or face-to-face visit.

The house list is a very significant asset of any organization. Keep building it and look after it.

Timing:

An imperfect letter sent out on time is better than a perfect letter sent three weeks late. Set a schedule and stick to it.

Do not let a committee or group of independent volunteers or staff members review and comment on the wording of a letter. This will always accomplish nothing more than missing mailing deadline dates and producing a letter that looks like it was (badly) written by a committee.

You can never catch up on lost income from a mailing that goes out late. If a mailing is two weeks late going out, you simply say goodbye to two weeks of income. Do not let this happen.

All sorts of self-appointed experts will tell you that donors and supporters will be turned off if they get too many letters. Ignore these claims. Track the response to every letter sent. Test on how frequently you can send them out to maximize net income. Do the math. Ten letters sent out every two weeks that produce an average ten percent response rate is far better for a campaign than five letters sent once a month that produce a fifteen percent response rate. If the response rate falls off sharply after increasing the frequency of mailings, then back off and send them less frequently until the optimum rate is reached.

A few years ago I was working for an international child sponsorship NGO. A disastrous hurricane hit one of the countries where we had several of our projects, damaging many of our facilities and devastating thousands of families. I urged that we send an immediate appeal letter to all of our child sponsors, something that we normally do not do since they were all giving monthly donations through the sponsorship program.

One of my colleagues strongly opposed the idea and argued that "We already ask these sponsors for money twelve times a year. That's enough. We will turn them off by asking for more." Fortunately the executive director was an accountant and could see the potential for net income. So we moved quickly and got the letter out while the story was still all over the news. The results were stunning. It was as if we had added an entire additional month of income. Moral: Politely ignore the naysayers, live with the occasional complaint, and keep asking for money when the opportunity is in front of you.

The content:

Letters must be personalized and read as if they are coming directly from one individual to another.

The words "I" and "you" should be used frequently. Do not use "our organization," "our campaign," or similar impersonal plural identifiers any more than is absolutely necessary.

Small mailings should be hand signed by the CEO. If it is a large mailing, the signature should be printed as if it were hand written.

Sometimes it may be appropriate for someone other than the CEO to sign the letter. Celebrity signatories have been shown to have little effect on improving the response unless the celebrity is somehow directly connected to the issue that the letter is all about (e.g., a retired general could write about national security or terrorism. A childhood cancer survivor could write about the need for more cancer research and services).

Signatures should always be in blue ink.

Large prospect mailings can use an impersonal salutation of "Dear friend" or "Dear member of our community" or something similar.

House mailings should always have a personalized name and address at the opening of the letter and a personalized salutation.

Example:

Organization's Letterhead

Date

Mr. John Doe

123 Main Street

Springfield, NJ 12345

Dear John: (*or* Dear Mr. Doe:)

Body of letter

Decisions to respond to fundraising letter are based on *emotions*, not cold rational logic. To get people to respond to a letter, it must engage their emotions.

Letters that produce warm and fuzzy feel-good emotions in the reader may create a positive feeling towards the organization but they will not get the reader to write and mail a check nearly as effectively as those that produce *negative* emotions. Feel-good letters can be sent occasionally in order to lift the spirits of your supporters and donors, but they should never become the predominant element in a direct mail program.

Like it or not, the negative emotions that best deliver check-writing are guilt, fear, anger, and pity. The content of a fundraising letter needs to leave the reader feeling one or two of these emotions.

The opening five lines of a letter must grab the reader emotionally. Otherwise the letter is not likely to be read.

The issue that forms the theme of the letter must not just be emotional; it must be pertinent to the emotions of the reader. For example, opening a new clinic for care of the elderly in County A will be emotionally important to residents of Country A, but it will likely be much less significant to those living three hundred miles away in County B.

The issue of the letter should be timely. Fighting apartheid in South Africa may have been important in the 1990's It's not today. If at all possible the issue of a letter should be having some current play in the media.

Caution: Don't be so tied to current events that the letter is rendered out of date within two or three days of mailing it. The response will be gone.

Another caution: Your letters along with all of your campaign materials will be read by your competition and the media. Never say anything that could be twisted and distorted to make you look either clueless or bigoted.

Use a Courier font to make the letter appear like it was written on a typewriter rather than a word-processor. (Sounds dumb, but testing has shown that this font gives a better response than Times New Roman, Arial or other popular MS Word fonts.)

Use short paragraphs. Five lines average – seven at most.

Keep sentences short. Use short familiar words. Direct mail letters are not the place to show off your literary skills.

The average age of the person who reads through a direct mail letter and responds will be 60+. So write the letter as if carrying on a conversation with a person in that age group. Do not use youth lingo or references to cultural events that you would have to be under thirty to understand. Never try to appeal to twenty-somethings. This age group may be wonderful as volunteers or for running fundraising events, but they don't read letters.

The P.S. following your signature is the most read and therefore the most important part of the letter. In two or three lines it needs to summarize the theme of the letter and repeat the call to action (i.e. send in a donation). Some self-appointed experts will tell you that a P.S. is cheesy. Ignore these people. Add a P.S. all the time.

The same self-appointed experts will say that nobody today reads a long letter and that every letter needs to be on only one page. This is nonsense from people who do not know what they are talking about (regardless of how nice and well-intentioned they are). It has been proven time and time again that a long letter produces a better rate of response than a short letter. Four pages (two pieces of paper written on both sides) is a minimum, except for occasional short memos sent as brief reminders to established donors.

The usual format for the content of an appeal letter is: a) an emotionally grabbing introduction; b) anecdotes or researched evidence of some problem that provokes an emotional response, like outrage, from the reader; c) how *you* are going to fix the problem; and

d) asking the reader to get involved and be part of the solution by sending in a donation.

A common technique is the inclusion of a brief – three questions – survey that asks the donor for his or her opinion on some current issue and send back the response. Such a survey can be used for both prospect and house mailings. The same goes for asking prospective donors to sign a petition.

Longer letters are particularly important when appealing to first time donors.

Prospect letters should contain lots of information related to whatever is the theme of the letter. *The more you tell the more you sell.*

Best advice? Gather together all the direct mail appeal letters received from charities, political campaigns, religious organizations, etc. Look at how they design their letters. If they seem to you to be really effective, they probably are. Copy them. But remember, copying verbatim from one source is called plagiarism. Copying with a few modifications from numerous sources is called creativity.

The Ask:

Remember . . . if you don't ask, you don't get.

Some experienced direct mail writers like to make a reference to the ask in the early paragraphs of a letter rather than leaving it to the end. You can try this, but anybody who opens a letter from a non-profit organization and starts to read it knows that an appeal is coming.

The best results come when the amount being asked for is directly related to some sort of unit that the campaign needs in order to win.

For example:

"Every gift of $50 will provide one month of life-saving anti-retroviral medicine to a child born with HIV-AIDS. $300 will help keep that child alive and healthy for six months." You get the idea.

Restate the ask at least two or three different ways. Use at least half a page to keep making it.

Tie the donation to something tangible, something relevant to the donor and laden with emotional content.

Enclosures:

It is common to include some sort of insert along with the letter, the reply coupon, and the return envelope. Do not use more than one insert per letter.

"Lift notes" consisting of a half-page note from some well-known and credible person endorsing the organization or cause are used often. These usually include a picture of the signer and a printed readable signature. The message should clearly state that the signer endorses the campaign, has made a personal donation to the campaign, and urges the reader to join him or her in doing the same.

You can also make occasional use of a copy of a newspaper clipping that highlights the issue you are raising funds for.. Or you can insert copies of a recent print ad. Or you can use a good quality photograph that shows something about the issue of the appeal. Sending photos beyond a snapshot size usually requires the addition of a cardboard stiffener so that the photo will not get damaged, along with a "Do Not Bend" notation on the envelope. These factors will add to the cost of the mailing but may also increase the response rate. Again: *test, test, test.*

Many organizations will also make occasional use of a premium – something intended to increase the response rate and the average amount of the donation. Personally signed copies of a book written by the CEO or founder of the organization work well and have been offered in return for every donation of $100 (or $75, or $50).

Any premium offered has to be honored and fulfilled immediately upon receiving the donation tied to it. Sour feelings and possibly even bad publicity will come from premiums that were offered but not fulfilled until weeks or months later.

The response inserts:

The response form and return envelope are essential items. Nothing goes out without them. This applies to *everything you send out.*

Every response form should look personal. Many use a personal letter format, such as:

Dear Dr. Gary:

YES! I want to help you defeat childhood cancer. Enclosed is my donation of . . .

Insert check off boxes for various gift amounts, including a blank one marked "Other" that the donor can fill in with his or her designated gift amount. Some direct mail specialists claim that you start with the high end amount and descend, others advise to you start low and grow. It probably doesn't matter.

The lowest option offered should be the average gift you expect to receive from the appeal. If you realistically expect, based on past results, to get an average gift of $20, then do not include a box for $15. The $20 box should be the lowest.

It is strongly urged that the recipient's name and address be printed on the response form *exactly as it appears in your donor database.* This will help greatly in record keeping and avoid the plague of creating multiple addresses and hence duplicate mailings for the same donor. It's also a lot easier to read than a donor's handwritten name and address.

Some larger campaigns have gone to using a barcode along with the name and address. This looks a lot less personal but it makes large batches of donations much easier to sort and enter accurately.

Always include a place where a donor can add his or her phone number and email address and ask the donor to enter them. These are very valuable for making future contact with the donor.

Most campaigns use a standard #6 return envelope with the name and address of the *person* in your organization to whom it is being sent.

There is not much difference in the economic efficiency of leaving the place for a stamp blank (most people have stamps) or using a postage-paid reply envelope. For high-end very personalized appeals or invitations to fundraising events, consider affixing an actual stamp on the return envelope.

What should the package look like?

All mailing packages should be of acceptable business quality but not overly glossy.

Basic 20 lb. 8 ½" x 11" paper will do for prospect mailings and can be printed on both sides without bleeding through from one side to the other.

Upgraded paper and envelope stock can be used for house mailings, and is particularly appropriate for specially targeted mailings to higher-end donors.

Event invitations should look like wedding invitations with RSVP envelopes, and they should include instructions for doing the RSVP by phone or Internet.

Have a graphic designer put together a letterhead that looks good. Use the same letterhead design consistently.

All of your mailings should look somewhat alike but always look personal, as if they came from a friend.

The body of the letter should not look cluttered. There needs to be a lot of white space and full margins at the top, bottom, and sides. Save trees some other time.

The envelope:

The goal is to make sure that the recipients open the envelope instead of just dumping it along with all the junk mail they receive.

With a few exceptions, direct mail appeals use a standard #10 envelope.

The best results are achieved using window envelopes with the name and address of the donor appearing in the window. People are more likely to open these envelopes because they look like they might be a bill.

Personalized addresses on envelopes should always be used for house mailings. If you do not want to use a window envelope, it is much better, although more time consuming, to hand-match a personalized letter with an envelope that is printed with the same address.

If using labels, transparent labels work better than white ones.

If sending a small number of highly personalized letters to high-end donors, you might want to ask a volunteer party of women to hand-write the name and address on the outside envelope. (This is not sexist. Men are just way too illegible).

Messages can be printed on the outside of the envelope. Check with the local USPS to determine where on the envelope and how large such messages can be. One or two lines that serve as teaser copy or convey urgency may be effective. Do not let it become cluttered.

Many campaigns will make use of an emergency look to the envelope by using yellow and black or universal orange. This works *occasionally*. Done too often it gets old, and there has to be a real *emergency*, like a response to a natural disaster. Do not cry wolf too often.

Live stamps work better than a franked stamp from a postage meter, but they cost significantly more to affix and use for obvious reasons.

When possible, the return address should include the name of a person, not just the organization. Use the name of the CEO, the signing celebrity, or even the honorary chair of a special campaign.

The Thank-You response:

Thank-you letters must be sent out as soon as possible after you receive a donation. Two weeks is the maximum. The same day or next day is way better.

In addition to expressing your thanks and appreciation the thank-you letter should note the amount of the gift received and the particular purpose for which it was given and should assure the donor that it is being put to use immediately for that reason.

It's okay to have a staff member hand-sign the thank-you letters but they should be clearly state that they are signed on behalf of the CEO or the organization or the celebrity in whose name the appeal letter was sent..

All thank-you mailings should include another response form and a reply envelope. You might (or might not) want to include a follow-up ask for an additional donation. Many campaigns say nothing except thank-you but get a lot of second donations by just including a reply form and envelope.

If someone sends you a large donation – $200 or more – then they should also get a thank-you phone call, ideally on the day the donation was received. Again, a staff member can do this. The message over the phone should be enthusiastic, sincere and short. Do not ask for another donation over the phone at this time.

Thank them before you bank them.

Donor database management:

I have included this paragraph under in the Direct Mail section since that is where the bulk of most non-profit donations still originate. But you must include *all* donations from all sources – personal contact, events, mail, telephone, Internet, TV, print ads . . . everywhere – in the donor database. Doing so is should be demanded by your auditors and is absolutely necessary if you want to do effective fundraising.

Record all donations in a database immediately upon receiving them. Do not let this function pile up.

Use a recommended commercial donor management software program. Do not just enter names and data into Excel.

The gold standard of fundraising software is *Raiser's Edge* by Blackbaud Inc. (www.blackbaud.com). It is likely more than is needed for a smaller organization. You can also check out DonorQuest (www.donorquest.com), a much less costly product that is particularly good for large direct marketing programs. Just make sure that there is a good database program and that your donor data is entered as soon as possible after you receive it.

A selected list of available programs, varying from the basic to the highly sophisticated can be found at:

http://idealware.org/articles/few-good-donor-management-systems

An exhaustive list can be found at:

http://www.capterra.com/fundraising-software

Many of the programs listed there will allow you to download a test version. If you do not currently have a program or do not like the one you have, spend a couple of hours and become familiar with the ones on the market, and then choose one and make it work for your organization.

Chapter Ten - Telemarketing

Nobody likes getting telemarketing calls.

Almost all successful campaigns, especially larger ones, use telemarketing in some way or other.

Why? Because it works. Not as well as it did a decade ago, but still very useful in a turnaround campaign.

The upsides of telemarketing are:

Immediate feedback; Within an hour on the phones you will know if an appeal is working or not. If it isn't, you can stop and fix it before you spend a fortune. This is not possible with direct mail where you only know how well you're going to do after sending out your packages.

Higher prospect response rate: Typically a good prospect mailing will achieve a 1–2 percent response. A prospect campaign by phone will achieve a 5–8 percent response rate. You can build a donor database far faster using the phone than the mail.

Higher house response rate: Typically a house mailing will deliver a 10–15 percent response rate. A telemarketing call to known donors will get 33–40 percent response, with a much higher rate for reactivating lapsed donors who used to support you but have stopped doing so.

The telephone can reach more young donors than direct mail.

Your callers get feedback from your donors on the organization and the campaign issues. Such information is very valuable and can be fed back to your turnaround campaign planners.

Callers can ask donors for their email addresses and record them. Some telemarketing software permits callers to send an email to potential donors while on the phone, either connecting them to your website or passing along an email piece that extols the goodness of your cause and organization.

Contact addresses can be confirmed and corrected over the phone.

Skilled callers can coax a higher donation from a donor.

Phone campaigns may have a higher overhead cost than mail campaigns, but because of the much higher response rates, the net income after the phone campaign is usually much more than after a mail campaign to the same donors.

The downsides of using outbound telemarketing are:

Voters and donors don't like getting called. So you can't call them as often as you can mail to them.

With mail, you can control the entire message down to the last comma. But even with very well-trained and closely supervised callers, you can never be sure that what is being said is what you want said. When you place thousands of calls you can be sure that at least a couple of them are not going to go well.

It's expensive. Large-scale prospect calling will cost at least 100 percent of what is given in first time prospect donations. Calls to your house donor list will cost between 33–66 percent of what is donated.

Serious caution on the use of call centers:

Some self-serving, unethical media reporters love attacking non-profits that use call centers for their telemarketing campaigns. In pursuit of a byline and a false reputation for standing up for the public interest these creeps will knowingly and deliberately mislead their readers by distorting the return to a charity from a telemarketing program.

All professional fundraisers are fully aware that any direct marketing program that is aggressively acquiring new donors by prospecting either by phone, by direct mail, or even by email will have very high overhead costs. Direct mail prospecting will often cost in excess of one hundred percent of the income received, and telemarketing campaigns will usually cost ninety percent since that is the limit allowed by many state governments.

Of course neither mail nor phone prospecting exist in a vacuum. They are part of an integrated system of donor acquisition and cultivation. Donors are acquired at a very high overhead cost are then followed up with house mailings and phone calls at a much lower cost per dollar received. Many of these donors are upgraded to monthly giving, where the overhead cost is less than five percent. Some donors are cultivated for major gifts, and a few for estate gifts. Some will attend the charity's events and make subsequent contributions through that opportunity.

The net cash received from direct marketing fundraising is also then leveraged through its use as the match for grants from foundations or government funding bodies and for the acquiring and shipping of very valuable gifts-in-kind.

Over a period of a few years these activities develop into an integrated fundraising system with an overall overhead ration of less than thirty percent and often less than twenty percent.

Those reporters with even an ounce of journalistic integrity understand how this works and would never mislead their readers, viewers, or listeners by isolating only one component of a fundraising system – telemarketing – and misrepresent it as representative of a charity's overall fundraising program. Those lacking it will.

Many individual fundraising activities will have high overhead costs. A large gala banquet or concert may gross over a quarter million dollars in income. But after the costs of renting the venue, paying for the advertising, food, performers, insurance, security, and so on the net might be less than $50,000. Such a single event would generally be considered a great success even though the costs were eighty percent of the total income.

Similarly a charity second-hand shop that receives donations of used goods will do very well to net back to the charity twenty percent of the overall income from sales. The rest will go towards space rental and occupancy costs, advertising, payroll, and administration.

Yet no pseudo-investigative reporters attack these types of fundraising activities.

The reason that telemarketing is so vulnerable to attack is also because of one of its greatest advantages, the turnkey services delivered by the consulting company that operates the call center. For a direct mail prospect campaign the fundraising consultant's fees for his or her creative writing and management services may be equivalent to fifteen percent of the overall costs. However another ten percent will be paid directly to a list broker, forty percent to USPS or Canada Post for stamps, forty percent to the printing and lettershop, and another ten to fifteen percent for the caging and data entry and transfer. But with telemarketing the call center provides all of these services. As a result there is just one payee, not six. That one private sector contractor ends up with ninety percent of the income from the campaign, and that is what makes telemarketing a very easy target for unscrupulous media scum.

Trust me on this one. I wear the scars of having helped non-profits raise huge amounts of net cash through telemarketing programs only to see those campaigns deliberately distorted by the media. Lesson learned? Never raise funds *only* from call center telemarketing, and if at all possible, distribute the costs of large campaigns through several different expense lines.

However, to do an effective telemarketing campaign, you really do need a sophisticated outbound call center with predictive dialers and an affiliated lettershop that can send out pledge collection packages within twenty-four hours of securing a pledged donation on the phone. Even very large organizations cannot do this in-house.

You need to use a very competent and reputable telemarketing company. There are a lot of regulations affecting telemarketing and *Do Not Call* lists, and they vary widely. You call center has to be in compliance or you could get into trouble.

Unless you are running a small local organization, do not attempt to do mass telephone fundraising yourself, especially when trying to acquire new donors. It's a tough job. Volunteers hate it.

Trained callers will achieve far better results than volunteers. The logistics are daunting. Hiring, training and firing your own paid telemarketers is a miserable way to spend your time. Don't do it.

Most telemarketing firms tend to lean either to the left of the right politically and usually do calling for one side or the other of the political spectrum as well as for non-profits. Few, if any, are bipartisan. If your cause is generally perceived to have political overtones then it is best to find a telemarketer that has a history of effective work for organizations that are on the same side of the political aisle as you are. Their management and their callers will be more comfortable with your cause and will perform better as a result. Check references.

Any contract you negotiate with a call center needs to have a break-even provision included that guarantees you will never end up owing more money to the call center than they raised for you. Really good shops will be willing to apply this guarantee to prospect calling all by itself. No competent set of callers can lose money calling recent past donors, so no guarantee for that segment is needed.

Most sophisticated call centers will offer a turnkey service, providing not only the calling but also the printing of pledge collection materials, mailing, caging, data entry, reminder mailings, daily (perhaps weekly) reporting of results, and daily (or weekly) downloading of donor data into your database. Unless you are running a very large and sophisticated organization and can do all of these functions yourself, accept the offer but note the caution given above on the reporting of your cumulative overhead costs.

As with direct mail, the list is crucial. Some call centers maintain their own internal database and can extract names of potential donors they believe are likely to be responsive to your appeal. Or you can rent lists from list brokers that logically would be appropriate to your organization. As with direct mail, test a few hundred random names from the list and analyze results before rolling out.

You can and should call telephone donors regularly. Once a year is NOT sufficient. Three to four times a year is normal. Five times is the maximum unless there is some sort of emergency reason for calling. More than once every two months will generate push-back from those being called.

Make sure that an appointed staff member has the authority to edit and sign-off on all scripts, back-up information, and printed pledge collection materials. Do not assign this task to a committee. Use the advice of your call center staff in drafting the script. Non-profit communications directors, board members, and even the CEO always want to say too much. Remember, on a telemarketing call the caller has about fifteen to twenty seconds to capture the interest of the listener. So keep it short.

As with direct mail, decisions made on the phone to make a donation are overwhelmingly *emotional*, not hard-nosed rational. Your appeal has to have some punch.

Do not offer to mail out information to someone who says they have to read all about the organization and cause before agreeing to make a donation. Ninety-five percent of these people will never send in a donation after receiving the mail package. The costs of providing this service will kill you.

Instead have the caller ask the listener to write down the organization's website address and take a look.

The way you get them is the way you keep them:

People who respond to prospect direct mail campaigns will also respond to telephone calls especially if there is some sort of urgent basis for the phone campaign. But . . . eighty-five percent of those who are contacted originally through the telephone will *never* respond to direct mail.

You can test sending mailings to your phone donor list, but the response rate will not likely exceed fifteen percent even after several attempts.

Younger donors will answer their phone. Many of them do not have landlines, so it is important to find some way to get their cell phone numbers.

You get them by asking for them. Always ask everybody to register for everything you do – events, rallies, workshops . . . whatever – and ask for their cell phone numbers and email addresses at that time.

Feed all names, addresses, and phone numbers into your donor database manager and call center as soon as you get them and have people called within a few days after having attended an event or having been contacted by one of your staff or volunteers.

Always try to secure phone donations on a credit card and then process those donations immediately. Your fulfillment rate on a credit card is usually about ninety-five percent (with about a five percent decline rate). The rate on those who receive subsequent pledge collection packages in the mail is going to be more like forty to sixty percent for prospecting (depending on the lists being called) and seventy-five percent on house campaigns. Some people will refuse to give their credit card over the phone, but ask anyway and offer whatever assurance you can provide to assuage their fears about security.

But then make very sure that the credit card data *is absolutely secure.* Many organizations and call centers deliberately erase all credit card data after processing the donation just to avoid ever having it stolen and misused. Any instance of having mass files of your campaign donors' credit card information fall into the wrong hands will be a very bad thing for your organization.

If your donor base is large enough it should be segmented into standard and high-end donors. Standard donors might be asked to donate beginning at $200, whereas high-end donors can be asked for donations beginning at $1000. Use experienced and effective callers for the high-end segment.

Pre-authorized monthly donors: As I noted earlier, monthly giving has become the most cost-effective means of direct marketing. If someone has given to your campaign twice in the past year and given over $35 each time, that donor is an excellent prospect for upgrading to a pre-authorized contribution level. Such a donor should be contacted as part of a special campaign using some of your best callers. The call is placed as a soft thank-you for previous donations and then the donor is told about the most efficient and effective way to help. For example: "Mrs. Smith, how would you feel about spending just $2 a day to help us provide more care for children with cancer?" You get the idea. A $2-a-day donation works out to $730 a year. That's a very significant donation and very few people will ever agree to make a single donation of that amount. But at $2 a day, they can do it.

Do these upgrading campaigns systematically. Do them two or three times a year to all those who have passed the criteria for being called. Process these credit cards on the same day every month. One month before the expiration date of the card, send an email asking for the new date. If there is no response, then make a phone call. Keep trying until you get the new date.

Losing a monthly donor just because of the expiration date is dumb.

As noted above in the section on personal telephone fundraising, Caller ID is the bane of telemarketing. Make sure the number that appears is not an 800 number or one that is Unknown or Blocked. It should be a number with an area code and three first digits that are in or close to the area of the person being called. If possible to arrange, the name displayed should be that of a senior staff person, the CEO or the person actually making the call. If you cannot use an individual's name then use the name of your organization.

Chapter Eleven – The Internet

During the past several years, non-profit organizations in the US and Canada have reported exceptional growth in the amount of donations received online.

But Internet fundraising still accounts for less than ten percent overall of all non-profit donations. It is absolutely *not* a replacement for face-to-face fundraising, events, or direct mail or telephone appeals.

And, it's time consuming. And it can be an expensive waste of money.

You have to have a website and a Facebook page. It's time to learn to Tweet. You have to be able to receive donations through the Internet and keep in contact with donors and volunteers through social media. But you had better be smart about it.

Guidelines:

Put up a good website. If you don't have experience in website design and management, go and look at several sites from other organizations, pick the one you and your team like best, and tell your website designer to make you one like it.

Get a professional website designer/manager. Do not let the geek friend of your high school-aged son do it for free. The cost of site designs has fallen incredibly in the past few years. Most of the software used by designers is available either free as open source or for a minimal cost.

Potential donors must be driven to your site from another medium. That's the way the Internet works. So your URL has to appear everywhere – on your letters, your TV ads, your event invitations, your phone pledge collection forms . . . everywhere.

The look of the site has to be similar to the look of the rest of your organization's materials.

The site URL needs to be unique, easy to remember and directly connected to the organization's name.

Get help with Search Engine Optimization (SEO) so that whenever someone types the name of your cause into Google or Bing, your site comes up on the first page, preferably on the top half.

Never forget to renew your URL registration or you could find that a poacher has grabbed it and is demanding a large fee to give it back to you.

Spend the few dollars necessary to register the most popular alternative names of your site. Also register the *.net, .org, .info, .us* addresses.

The site must be kept current and be interesting. An excellent fundraising appeal on a boring site is a boring appeal.

Keep on featuring real stories about real people and how they feel and have been affected by events related to your cause and by your programs delivered to them. Start the story on the home page with a *read more* link to the rest of the story.

Never forget that a good story *always* trumps a rational argument or list of statistics.

Ideally you should be posting new information on your site every day. Once a week is the absolute minimum.

A visitor to the site must immediately see that you have a compelling narrative to share with them. Your message needs to be strong, clear, and consistent.

Remove announcements of events and references to items in the news as soon as they have passed.

Keep items on your home page and your news page short with links to the rest of the story for those who might want to read more. Most won't.

Use photos and graphics. If possible, integrate a series of brief videos. Video messages from your CEO or celebrity spokesperson should have a conversational tone, no shouting, lots of eye contact - as if the speaker were sitting across the living room and talking to you.

How to raise funds on the Internet:

Internet fundraising is not a stand-alone program. It is an integrated part of an overall fundraising program. People who read your letters will often look at your site. So will those who are invited to events. They may choose to donate online rather than through the medium by which they were initially contacted.

The same goes for telephone pledge payments. So treat the Internet as one of several ways through which you are communicating with all of your donors, not just an isolated segmented group who will only get to know about you online.

As with all fundraising, you have to *ask* for the donation, and this request needs to appear throughout the website. In the text portion you need to insert a "Johnson Box" into the body of the text with a headline telling readers to donate now by clicking the link to the donation page.

The "Donate Now" button should be on your home page at the top right corner (best) or top left. It should be in a distinctive color and easily readable. Use a headline on the button instead of just "Donate Now." For example: *Help Fight Childhood Cancer: Donate Now!*

Similar Donate Now buttons should appear on every page of your website.

When donors click on a Donate Now button they should be taken immediately to the donation page. It should have several options for donations but should strongly feature a pre-authorized monthly contribution with a headline indicating that this is a special level of donation and the best way to support the organization. Suggest a reasonable monthly amount and provide a place for the donor to fill in his or her desired monthly amount.

Donors should also have the option of making a one-time donation instead and filling in the amount he or she wishes to donate at that time.

We suggest offering several levels of donation and relating the gift to a tangible cost of the service your organization provides, e.g., *Your $100 will cover the cost of a scientist carrying out one hour of research towards the cure for childhood leukemia.* Provide appropriate similar connections for various gift levels.

Do *not* just use the standard version of PayPal to process the donation. If you do, then all you will receive is the donation and the email address of the donor.

It is imperative that you capture all of the contact information from the donor. You must also have a section below the donation selection where the donor fills in name, full mailing address, phone number, cell phone number, and email address.

Insert a privacy policy note stating that your organization will never sell, trade, or share contact information, if that is indeed your intent.

But also include a disclosure stating that all donors will receive subsequent contact from the organization by email, mail, or phone. If you feel it necessary, you can include a check-off box in which the donor clearly opts *not* to be contacted again, but you really don't want any of your donors to tell you that, because you really want to be able to contact them again and again in the future.

You will also need a final confirmation button to make sure that the donor has understood that he or she is making a donation by credit card to your organization. Some e-commerce sites include a "Confirm Sale" page that reconfirms the transaction. A good e-commerce site designer will be able to guide you through the process.

Your site software must be connected to your database so that all of the information provided can be downloaded into whatever database software you are using.

Your software should be able to process a credit card donation and immediately send a confirmation back to the donor's email thanking him or her.

Test the process extensively before going live with your site. Make sure it works.

Sign up for Google Analytics and use it to monitor the site. Make adjustments as needed.

Making Internet fundraising work better:

Visit a lot of other non-profit websites. Copy all the great ideas you can find.

Make your changes quickly and monitor both the donation results and the Google Analytics information.

Your site designer must include a content management system that allows your staff person to make immediate changes in the site. You cannot be left in a position where the only person that can make changes to the site is the site manager or hosting service.

Keep it simple. Do *not* make the site visitor or potential donor have to think and puzzle his or her way through your site. Donating online has to be easy or it won't happen.

Some organizations append a blog to the website. Blogs templates like WordPress are very easy to update by almost anybody.

The story you give to the reader must be compelling. So must the reason for making a donation. Internet donations depend on immediate emotional responses.

Do *not* place a lot of complicated background information on the main pages of the site. If you want to have a copy of the latest government foreign aid policy document available for your site visitors, just provide a link to it. But do not strongly advertise links that take the viewer outside of your site. When that happens the likelihood of getting a donation dwindles because most viewers who leave your site through a link will not return to make a donation.

Engage the donor by using some sort of survey to be filled out, or letting him or her send in comments or an email back to the CEO. Use a "Call to Action" that instructs the donor to *do something* now about whatever is the most pressing issue of the day. Give them the email address, office phone number, and mailing address of a House or Senate Committee Chair or Governor's office or Mayor and tell them what to communicate to that person. Try to get them to do something while they are still online on your site. But do not let these functions detract from the donation process.

Enhancing the fundraising:

Offer something *FREE*, such as an e-book written by the CEO with a title like *A Child in Africa*. It can be a simple ten-page document in which the CEO talks about his or her latest experience related to your cause. If you don't have an e-book like that, *write one!* When site visitors click on the *FREE* button they are taken to the contact information page (also referred to as the "squeeze page") and asked to submit their names, addresses, phone numbers, and email addresses. Only when this information has been entered can they download the free item.

Getting this information will permit you to make subsequent contact with these people by email, mail, or phone to solicit donations.

If you have a fundraising event and get (as you must) the contact information of those who attended, send them an email the next day with a link to pictures that were taken at the event. The email you send should have a link to your website and the recipients should land on a page with content referring specifically to the event they attended, along with another donation button. Then they should be able to click through to the photos. Use a site like Flickr that is easy to post photos on. If there is any video of the event, post it on YouTube and send them to that site as well.

Try an online auction. If you can obtain anything signed by a celebrity put it up for auction. Offer Broadway show tickets, rounds of golf at a great course, signed copies of books, travel to a resort . . . anything that you and your staff would personally love to be able to win or buy at auction. There are companies that specialize in running online auctions. Use them. But make sure that every participant signs in with contact information and that you get that data.

Have a page on the site on which the donors to the organization are listed and thanked again online. Before doing this, however, make sure that the donor agrees to having his or her name posted. Give special recognition to those who made major gifts, those who are pre-authorized monthly donors, and those that have named your organization in their will.

Offer some sort of web-based premium in return for a donation, such as a special seal or logo that the donor can post on his or her own website, Facebook page, or email signature..

Set up a paid membership program where members get a newsletter every month and VIP invitations to events.

Do everything you can to assist in having your message go viral. Tell your donors and supporters to reTweet or email your message, video, or YouTube link out to all their friends.

Don't worry too much about whether or not your exact controlled message is going out accurately. You can't control that in real life and you can't control it on the Internet. Just make sure that your URL is appended to everything you send so that those who have questions can go to your site and find out your message directly.

Using the Internet seems much cheaper than direct mail, telephone, TV, and fundraising events. But it can be very time consuming. So discern quickly who you are reaching by using the Internet, how many of them are responding, and what sort of donations they are making. If it appears to be working, then keep getting better at it. If it does not have the same return for dollars and hours invested as other forms of fundraising, govern yourselves accordingly.

Fundraising by email:

Sending emails is far cheaper (it's almost free) than sending letters in the mail or making phone calls. But the response rate is much lower.

As a result, many campaigns use a "1, 2, 3 punch" where they start with an email appeal, followed quickly by a direct mail appeal to all those who did not respond to the email, and then followed by a telemarketing call to all those who did not respond to either the email or the letter.

Eighty percent or more of those who are going to respond by email will do so within a few days. So after one week you can remove the names of those who did respond and send a letter to the rest.

Fifty percent of those who are going to respond to a letter will usually do so within fourteen days of the letter's having been mailed. This is referred to as the "doubling date." It will vary depending on the class of postage used on the mailing. Lower class postage takes longer to arrive and so the doubling date is later. By one week past the doubling date seventy-five percent of those who are going to respond have likely done so. At that point you can remove their names from the list and have your call center phone the rest. There will be some overlap from one phase to the next. This will only be an issue for those getting phone calls who have recently mailed their donations. Just have the callers apologize nicely and move on.

Use a good email management software program (iConnect, Aweber, ConstantContact, or MailChimp). These allow you to track how many of your emails actually got delivered to the mailbox they were sent to and how many got opened and read. If the opening ratio is low, then you have to examine your program and make sure that your emails are sufficiently interesting and compelling so that they do get opened.

Whenever possible, use the first name, or first and last names, or the salutation and name of the person receiving the email in the email subject line. This helps get it opened.

Many emails now are being opened in either handheld devices or on email programs that permit the receiver to read not only the subject line but also the first two or three lines of the email message. This content is referred to as being "above the fold." You need to make the first few lines compelling. They have to trigger a response that will move the reader to open the message and read it.

Unlike direct mail appeals, email appeals are usually short. Most are just two or three brief paragraphs, with the last paragraph being the ask and the instruction to click on the link to make a donation. If there is more information it should be placed below the donate button so that anyone who wants can scroll down and read it. Or it should be linked from the email page to a page on the website.

Emails can be sent once a week. Some organizations and campaigns send as often as once a day. If the content is more like a short blog post on events of that day this can work, with an ask attached to the end of the message. Just asking for money every day without some interesting content along with it is a bit much. Regardless, you can email your donors more often than you can mail to them and way more often than you can phone them.

A video with a message from the candidate can be embedded in an email as long as it can be downloaded quickly. If it takes more than a few seconds for the reader to download the video, it will be lost.

As with all fundraising, the more personal the better. The donor's name should appear in the salutation of the message and possibly inserted once more in the body. A signature from the CEO or the person sending the email should be scanned and inserted at the end of the letter. A picture of your supporting celebrity or the CEO either in a posed setting, in action at an event, or talking to someone (e.g., students, seniors, children) can be embedded into the email at the end. However, adding these into an email will definitely slow down the opening of it. A surprising number of Americans and Canadians are still using dialup Internet services and photos take forever to download.

When an email donor clicks to donate, he or she needs to be taken to your site donation page and immediately asked to sign up as a monthly donor and then be given the same options for giving as anyone else who donates through your website. If your software is sufficiently clever, it will automatically display the contact information of the donor by reading the email address and pulling up the file. But if not, always ask for the contact information again. You may end up with duplicate entries in your database by doing so, but that's why you need to clean and purge your database regularly.

Many Internet campaigns for non-profit organizations now ask for a very small initial donation. Three dollars appears to be the most common request. There's a reason for doing so. Few if any of your email recipients are not in a position to send three dollars to a cause they believe in and the response rate to such a minimum appeal has proven to be the most effective. The goal, of course, is to secure a first donation, get full contact information about the donor, and then cultivate that donor over time for continuing and increasing repeat donations.

Prospecting by email:

Some organizations have done well renting massive email lists and sending out a prospect mailing. For this to work you need a good list – one that has a direct connection to likely donors, not one that some web crawler has put together – and you also need a very compelling subject line or your email will not get opened.

Spamming is against the law. Make absolutely certain that any list you rent has been cleared for receiving unsolicited emails from affiliated organizations or sponsors.

Always test a few thousand – maybe 5000 – email addresses before agreeing to rent the entire list. As with direct mail, if you can break even or come close on a well-designed market test, then you will achieve the same result on the rollout. If you lose a lot of money on the test then the full list isn't worth renting. Test several subject lines and content messages for the same list and pick the winner. The hotter an issue is in the media, the more likely your email to be opened and responded to.

Try using your supporting celebrity's name in the subject line. For example: *"John, a message to you from Brad Pitt."* Or just use the CEO's name.

Try to make your emails look attractive, personal, and easy to read. Some organizations use an old-fashioned Courier font and include a salutation and a traditional closing and signature. Occasional spots of color can dress it up, but don't overdo it.

Social media / Web 2.0:

All non-profit organizations need a Facebook page. If you don't know how to build one and how to attract "friends," just ask any child of a volunteer that is beyond grade six and they'll explain it to you.

Tweet. The tweets should be sent from your CEO or maybe from an associated celebrity. If not good at tweeting then have someone on staff do it for you under the name of the CEO. Get out at least one good tweet a day. Build your following.

Facebook, Twitter addresses, and blog sites are now usually appended to the signature line in every appeal and fund-raising letter. Keep these current and working.

Other social media sites such as LinkedIn, MySpace, YouTube, Flickr, and Instagram may also be useful as communication tools, but Facebook and Twitter are now essential.

Constantly be looking for like-minded people who can join your friends and followers lists. Post on your page several times a week, and once a week at a minimum. Read posts from your friends and send a comment back to them if what they have posted has anything to do you're your cause.

Always send a birthday greeting to all your friends and be sure to comment on any significant post noting an achievement (e.g., got married, new job, had a baby, child accepted to college . . . the usual stuff).

Facebook has not yet proven to be an effective place to do fundraising, but it is certainly very effective for finding prospective volunteers and potential future donors.

Make reference in your posts to your website, any recent videos on YouTube, any event coming up . . . whatever. Always ask your friends to share the information with their friends. If a piece of information or a video is sufficiently timely, clever, fascinating, or compelling it just may go viral and you will suddenly be in contact with many, many more people, and younger people, than all your TV ads and letters could ever hope to achieve.

Facebook ads are great for locating other people with similar interests in any specified geographic area. Try using them for advertising an event or even a Meet-Up group. Facebook ads can be tested for a few dollars, refined constantly to help you target the people you want to find, and then rolled out to whatever demographic you choose.

Also become proficient with Google AdWords. These are the small ads consisting of three lines and a URL that show up on the right hand side of a Google search. Again, they can be customized to find only those people who might be interested in supporting your campaign. Test them on a limited basis and, if they are working, roll them out.

Both Google and Facebook have online tutorials that will walk you through the process for writing, placing and paying for ads. It's not hard. Just make sure you limit the amount you are willing to spend each day during the test phase.

Fundraising on the Internet is a young and constantly developing field. New techniques are being tried, improved, or discarded all the time. Sign up to many different non-profit websites, RSS feeds, email newsletters, Facebook pages and Tweeters and watch what others are doing. Learn from the latest and cleverest techniques.

But do not forget, that giving money to a cause or organization regardless of the medium used is a personal and emotional act. One person asks another person to join the cause and help make a difference in the world. Your internet appeals have to reflect this principle.

Chapter Twelve – Consultants

Expert fundraising consultants can guide your non-profit out of its financial crisis. Poor ones will just dig you farther into a hole.

Over the past two decades fundraising consultants and consulting firms have come to play an increasing role in the management of non-profit campaigns. Their extensive professional knowledge and their experience have made them very valuable to many non-profit organizations.

Most consultants do not devote one hundred percent of their time to any one organization. Many will work on two or three or more campaigns at a time. There are general fundraising consultants, as well as consultants who specialize in direct mail, telemarketing, Internet, planned giving, major gifts, corporate campaigns, annual or capital campaigns, events, and door-to-door fundraising - just about any aspect of a fundraising program you can imagine . . . and then some you never thought of. Some work all alone. Some work for multi-million dollar consulting firms.

The most critical things to manage are the fees paid to fundraising consultants, the expectation of what is delivered, their expenses, and their authority. All of these areas can create problems for any organization, but if managed carefully can help to create a very successful campaign that is assisted by highly professional experts

Consultants who assist with paid media – TV, radio, direct mail, telemarketing, Internet advertising – will often receive an agent's commission or brokerage fee from the corporation with whom they place the work. For example: a direct mail consultant may charge your campaign a very reasonable $1500 for the creative work done in writing your letters. He or she will then place the letter with a printer and lettershop (sometimes the same place) which might charge the campaign $60,000 for printing, addressing, stuffing, postage, and mailing out a fundraising appeal letter to 100,000 people. If the postage portion is $29,000, then the rest of the costs combined would be $31,000. Your consultant may receive an agent's or broker's fee from the lettershop equal to fifteen percent of the total bill, or in the case of this example, $4650. In the construction industry this might be called a kickback. In media buying and direct marketing, it's how the business legally works.

It is often in the interest of the consultant to have your organization purchase as much telemarketing, direct mail services, and other media as possible and pay the highest rate possible since this is where they make the bulk of their income. This arrangement does create a potential conflict of interest since the greatest financial return to the consultant may not be in the best financial interest of your organization. Reputable professional fundraising consultants know that their true long-term best interests are in delivering to your campaign the best deal possible, since that way you will keep using them year after year. Less scrupulous consultants may gouge you for short-term gain.

So, hire slowly. Get proposals and interview several applicants. Check references. Look at the track record. Go with experience in any major contract.

Get it in writing. Work out a very detailed contract that covers everything you can think of. *You* should write the contract, not the consultant. Agree on everything and sign off before starting work together.

Fundraising consultants cost a lot. Good ones are worth every cent. Too many consultants will, like cooks, not only spoil the broth but can bankrupt the organization. Set a budget for paying consultants and stick to it.

Do not pay a fundraising consultant for advice and expertise you can get for free from your board members, advisors, staff, old hands, retired senior staff, and past volunteers.

Conversely, "don't buy a dog and do your own barking." Do not pay a consultant to do work and then have staff and/or volunteers duplicate the same tasks.

Always negotiate fees. Ask for discounts. Give rewards for success - a campaign that met or surpassed its goal - not just for work done or money expended. Fundraising consultants who belong to the AFP cannot work on the basis of commissions or any other type of fees related directly to performance, so find other ways that are acceptable to all parties of recognizing and rewarding those consultants if they deliver a successful fundraising campaign.

Some consultants are pure mercenaries and can provide excellent services to any organization, but these people are rare. Usually you will need to find a consultant who shares the convictions of the organization.

Many consultants are part of a network of professional associates who are also friends. Often if you hire one consultant he or she will begin lobbying for you to hire one of their highly recommended friends for another part of your campaign. If finding a consultant for that area of work was not in your Plan, don't do it. Stick to the Plan. Note, however, that some consultants have rather large egos and do not play well with other consultants who are not already their friends. Act accordingly.

You need to be specific concerning what you are paying a consultant to deliver. Every consultant should be able to offer expert advice almost immediately. You should not have to pay for them to do research and extensive study of your operation or learn all about the nature of fundraising for your particular cause before giving you the recommendations you need.

You should expect to pay for skills and expertise and the rapid delivery of high quality work. A direct mail consultant, for example, should be able to draft an effective fundraising letter on very short notice.

Consultants should be able to provide you with recommendations concerning service providers for your printing, TV and radio production, caterers, venues, etc. These recommendations should be made in the best interests of your organization, not of the consultant.

An experienced fundraising consultant will convey a credible sense of having seen it all before and will be able to warn you of potential pitfalls before they happen.

Within reason, your consultant meets with you according to your schedule, not his or her convenience. Do not hire a consultant that is already working for four or more other organizations.

Specify in the written contract what it is you expect from your consultant. If you expect a weekly meeting with members of your fundraising staff, put it in writing. If you expect specific deliverables, say so.

Specify the starting and the ending date of the contract.

Specify ownership of intellectual property and work product. If you are paying for it, it all belongs to you. This cannot apply to common professional knowledge or to a consultant's particular expertise, but it should apply to all work product created specifically for your campaign. There must be no restrictions on your future use of the work product.

Standard strict confidentiality clauses must be included.

Most consultants will require a non-circumvention broker protection commitment from a campaign. If they introduce your campaign to one of their suppliers, you cannot subsequently do an end run on the consultant and try to work with the same supplier for a reduced fee.

The method of payment must be specified. If it is a per diem, then the definition of a *day* must be written out. Do professional preparation days count? Or only days actually present and meeting with campaign leaders? What about travel days?

Will there be a bonus for a successful campaign? If so, what will it be?

Will the consultant be paid based on the overall costs of the work he or she oversees? If so, how much, and how will you control the gross costs?

When are invoices to be presented and when will they be due? Are any advances provided against fees? Against expenses?

Who can request and authorize additional consultant time? Will additional days be paid at the same rate?

Limits on what a fundraising consultant can contract in the name of the organization must be specified, and usually it is good to have strict restrictions. For most organizations all expenditures and contracts need to be signed off by either the CEO or the CFO; never a consultant.

Is the consultant authorized or expected to cover up-front costs such as postage or deposits from his or her own pocket? How and when will such payments be repaid?

Expenses must be limited. Unless you are working on a million dollar plus campaign for a major non-profit with one of the most qualified and successful fundraising consultancy firms in the country, you should not expect to pay outrageous expense claims. Consultants can stay in decent mid-range business hotels, travel economy class, rent mid-size cars, pay for their own booze, and eat for $60 a day or less. Make sure that these costs are restricted in writing and controlled. Require that all expenses be backed up by standard documentation.

It is always much more economical to hire locally so that you are not having to pay travel and accommodation expenses.

The process for the early termination of a contract must be spelled out. These terms must be perceived to be fair to both parties. If a consultant quits, he or she should give at least two weeks' notice. Some sort of penalty should be applied for quitting on the spot. If your campaign fires a consultant, there needs to be some sort of fair severance agreement unless it is clearly for cause.

The organization and the consultant must agree in advance on the expected deliverables. Do you expect face time? How much and with whom? Or are you content with telephone time? Email time? Are there reasonable targets for net income that you expect to reach by specific dates? Are there bonuses or penalties for exceeding or falling short of targets?

If you are using a consultant for media production and buying, how many ads are you contracting for? What is the projected schedule?

Caution: Fundraising campaigns are being driven more and more by professional contract staff and consultants. The good ones can deliver boatloads of donations and help achieve a highly successful turnaround campaign. The poor ones can't. Either type can cost a fortune.

The rescue and recovery phase of what had been a failing organization can be an intense time. Human emotions run high. Personalities can clash. An income target achieved at the cost of trampling the dignity and spirit of staff and volunteers who may be victims of a consultant's ego will be far harder to repeat next year. There are more than enough extremely capable fundraising consultants out there who can work well with your organization, fundraising staff, and volunteers. Choose *them*.

CONCLUSION

You are probably familiar with the story of Christopher Wren, one of history's greatest architects. Wren was commissioned to design and rebuild St. Paul's Cathedral in London after the Great Fire had leveled most of the city in 1666.

He prepared the plans for what is still today one of the most impressive churches ever built. During the construction phase Christopher Wren walked around the site observing and inspecting the progress. As he did he stopped and watched three bricklayers. He called out to each bricklayer, asking the same question: "What are you doing?"

The first bricklayer looked down on the architect, shrugged, and replied, "I'm just earning my living."

The second man said, "What does it look like? I'm building a wall."

The response of the third bricklayer was different. He gestured to the emerging structure and said, "I'm building a cathedral to The Almighty."

There will be many times when you, as someone engaged in turning around a worthy organization, may feel like all you are doing is firing marginal people, setting up chairs, licking stamps, or haggling with a call center over their fees. Much of the day-to-day business of organizational turnaround, we all have to admit, can be repetitive, uninspiring, and occasionally even discouraging.

So it is always good to stop and remind ourselves that we are not just earning our living, or trying to fix an organization. We are making it possible to continue to provide services to people in need – men, women, children and communities who depend on us. We are promoting those values of civil society that make America and Canada what they are today, and will continue to keep our countries and communities compassionate, caring and prosperous. We are "building a Cathedral."

And you and I are not alone. We are part of an enormous movement of like-minded people who are all doing similar work for the good causes. All over the continent men and women, young and old, of all walks of life, all faiths, and all countries of ancestry are making phone calls, writing letters, calculating returns on expenditures, and attending countless rubber chicken lunches. In doing so we are providing worthy non-profit organizations with the funds they need to provide those benefits that we know in our hearts and minds are infinitely worthwhile.

It has been said of people who care about working together to help those in need that they are *unknown on earth but well-known in heaven.*

All the best. Keep up the great work. It's worth it.

God bless.

About the Author

Craig Copland has been active in the non-profit sector for over forty years. He has been a volunteer, staff member, executive, CEO, and consultant and a member of over twenty boards of directors. He has "been around a long time and seen it all." Most of his work now is directed to helping conservative organizations in Canada and the US and he is the author of the much appreciated *2012 Conservative Election Handbook: Everything You Need to Know to Elect Conservatives to Public Office . . .from Dog Catcher to President,* which was distributed to over 7500 conservative candidates, as well as *Fundraising for Conservatives.* Regardless of his personal political convictions he has a profound respect for anyone who will take a public stance in support of their convictions, and this book, *Non-Profit Turnaround,* is a bi-partisan guide that will be useful to any organization that is struggling to have its finances repaired and its voice heard. He lives, works, and writes from New York, Vienna, and Toronto. He can be reached at **Craig@DonorClub.org.**

Made in the USA
Lexington, KY
02 October 2013